DEFINING CHRIST

The Book of Luke
in 88 Lessons

Tracy L. Brinson, D. Min.

Tracy L. Brinson
GOSPEL PUBLISHING

Perry, Georgia 31069

DEFINING CHRIST, Brinson, Tracy L.

First Edition

Tracy L. Brinson
GOSPEL PUBLISHING

Perry, Georgia 31069

Cover, Formatting and Proofing by:
Farley Dunn

ISBN: 978-1-7336794-0-4

Copyright © 2019 by Tracy L. Brinson

Contents

FOREWORD

I first met Dr. Tracy Brinson when we were both freshmen at Norman College in Georgia. Almost from the time we met we became personal friends. This friendship has lasted for more than fifty-six years.

After graduation from Norman College, Dr. Brinson continued his education at Samford University (B.A.), the Southern Baptist Theological Seminary (Master of Divinity), The University of Georgia, and earned the Doctor of Ministry Degree at Luther Rice Seminary.

Dr. Brinson has served faithfully as pastor of Southern Baptist churches in Georgia, Alabama and Kentucky and in key positions in denominational life, including serving as a member of the Executive Committee of the Georgia Baptist convention and as a trustee of Lifeway Christian Resources.

It has been my privilege to work with Dr. Brinson in many revivals and Bible conferences across the years. He has always done a great job. The passion of his heart is to preach God's Word and to lead people to a faith in Jesus Christ. I highly recommend this new phase of his ministry. The messages in this book will be helpful to anyone who will take them seriously.

My association with Tracy has taught me the truth of Proverbs 18:24. He is my brother in Christ, my partner in ministry and my golfing buddy. I can assure you that he is a much better teacher and preacher than he is a golfer.

Argin G. Floyd, Pastor

PREFACE

This book of studies on the Gospel of Luke started as a Wednesday night study class at First Baptist Church, Perry, Georgia, where I was serving as associate pastor, with care of senior adults and pastoral care. That was after 51 years of ministry as senior pastor in churches in Georgia, Alabama, and Kentucky.

For years, Luke has been my favorite book of the Bible. Little did it cross my mind that these studies might become a book. After many lessons had been prepared and taught, God led me to see that this study could become a book designed for pastors who had no formal education in a Bible college or seminary. Then I realized that it could become a resource for teachers of Bible classes, or for seekers of God who had a desire to study the Bible in greater depth, alone, or in small groups.

These are complete studies of Dr. Luke's gospel. The student could take this book, or any lesson in it, pray diligently, allow the Holy Spirit to guide, adding other thoughts, interpretations, applications, and illustrations. With this, one would have a bona-fide sermon or lesson.

The reader will soon see that this book is written from the belief that the Bible is authentic, inspired by God, infallible, and inerrant word of the living God. As a Southern Baptist pastor for 56 plus years, I continue to be in full agreement with "The Baptist Faith and Message," current version of June 14, 2000. This "statement" is a documented study of Baptists' primary doctrines.

This book is intended for churches of any size, or individuals. There is a special place in my heart for bi-vocational pastors and other bi-vocational ministers. My Daddy, Frank L. Brinson, likely the most humble man I've ever known, was from Swainsboro, Georgia. He was called by God at the age of 50 to become a pastor and preacher.

Daddy was from "the Great Depression" era of the 1920's and 1930's, who had a formal education up to about the 8th grade. By the grace and power of God, he availed himself of helpful Bible courses. God gave him what he needed to pastor and preach in several churches until he was about 85 years old.

There are no foot notes nor end notes. I sat with my Bible and sought my God with prayer and wrote these lessons, depending on the Holy Spirit for what is written. This work is credited to God in HIS many-splendored glory.

Dr. Tracy Brinson

ABOUT DR. TRACY L. BRINSON

I am a Christian [believer in Jesus Christ; born again; and I love the Lord].

I have pastored 10 churches over 57 years – in Georgia, Alabama, Kentucky.

Education: High School; Business College; AA in Junior College; BA at Samford University; Master of Divinity at Southern Seminary, Louisville, Kentucky; Doctor of Ministry at Luther Rice Seminary.

Retired now. My last job was as Associate Pastor of Sr. Adults at First Baptist Church, Perry, GA. My wife, Heather, and I live in Perry, Georgia.

ACKNOWLEDGEMENTS

My thanks to Rev. Argin G. Floyd, who wrote the foreword. He is my best friend, a devout and humble Christian, a great preacher of God's word for more than 60 years. He is an always-available counselor to me. No one could ask for a better friend.

———————

Thanks to Ms. Becky Millar, Pastor's secretary at First Baptist Church, Perry, Ga. She has been a gift to me from our Pastor, and most loyal to my requests in the typing of the manuscript, making suggestions regarding the book, correcting punctuation, and keeping in touch with the editor and me—not a little job.

———————

Pastor Jamie Powell has a calling to be a Pastor/Preacher. In his tenth year as pastor of First Baptist Church, Perry, Ga., he leads us well and is a great teacher and preacher. He allowed Becky to work on this project when time permitted. He is my pastor, a beloved man of God, a most efficient messenger of God's word.

———————

Lastly, thank you to my editor, Farley Dunn, of Three Skillet Publishing for working with me to bring this book into being.

Mr. Dunn is a fellow believer in Christ. After nearly a decade heading the elementary Sunday school department of a large Fort Worth church and 35 years in public education, he left the teaching field to start his publishing company. He has helped bring over 100 new books to the market and enjoys working with writers who are just getting their feet wet.

Mr. Dunn lives with his wife and numerous pets. He splits his time between his native Texas, his son's North Carolina home, and the mountains of North Georgia. When he can, he meanders to Maine for a week or two on the island of Vinalhaven, 12 miles out to sea, to clear his thoughts in the salty ocean breeze.

One day, Mr. Dunn vows, he'll head to Maine and plant his roots for all time. Until then, he has more books to publish, and he's ready to start his next one.

DEFINING CHRIST

Lesson 1

Introduction

Luke 1:1-25

I.   INTRODUCTION: (vv. 1-4)
   A. One of 4 gospels. Why?
   B. Luke, the author
      1. The only Gentile writer
      2. The "beloved physician"
      3. A missionary, working with the apostle Paul
      4. The author of which other New Testament book?
         Acts
   C. Purpose and Destination
      1. To write an orderly account of Jesus and the gospel
      2. Written to Theophilus
        a. A governor of a Roman province; a high official
           of the Roman Empire
        b. A gentile Christian
        c. A close friend of Luke
   D. Special emphases of Luke
      1. The prayer life of Jesus
      2. The people whose lives Jesus touched
      3. Fellowship Jesus had in the homes of people
   E. Stories found in Luke, only
      1. Gabriel's visit to Zechariah and Elizabeth
      2. The song of Mary
      3. Chapters 11-18 are exclusive to Luke.
      4. Parables of the prodigal son, the lost coin, the rich
         man and Lazarus, the Good

5. Samaritan, the penitent thief, and more

II.   <u>THE PROMISED FORERUNNER OF JESUS: JOHN, THE BAPTIST</u> (vv. 5-25)

   A. Major players

      1. Zechariah & Elizabeth

      2. Gabriel the angel

      3. John, the Baptist

   B. The Birth of John the Baptist (vv. 57-66)

      1. Imagine how Elizabeth felt. (vv. 57-61)

      2. Elizabeth knew his name in advance.

   C. John the Baptist

      1. Meaning of name "the grace of Jehovah"

      2. Was to be a "Nazarite" (v. 15)

      3. Will be great in God's sight (v. 15)

      4. Will be one who prepares the people for the Lord (vv. 16-17)

      5. At last, a real prophet

      6. Filled & empowered by the Holy Spirit

      7. Destined before birth (Isaiah 40:3-5)

Lesson 2

"Jesus and John the Baptist"

Luke 1:26-80

I. THE BIRTH OF JESUS FORETOLD (vv. 26-38)
    A. The sixth month after the announcement of John's birth
    B. Nazareth, a town of Galilee in Northern Israel
    C. The announcement of Jesus' birth to Mary by Gabriel, the angel
        1. Mary, a virgin, pledged (betrothed) to be married to Joseph
        2. Imagine, a greeting from God
        3. "Favor with God" means grace. (the unmerited favor of God)
        4. Mary troubled, and God's response (vv. 29-33)
            a. When God speaks it's very important.
            b. A common word from God, "Don't be afraid."
        5. The announcement
            a. Mary will have a baby.
            b. The son born will be the Messiah.
                i.   Son of the Most High
                ii. Will reign over Israel
                iii. Kingdom is eternal
    D. God's method of the birth (vv. 34-38)
        1. God will make it happen, a miracle.
        2. With God, "impossible" is never relevant.
        3. Mary's servant heart

II.   ELIZABETH'S RESPONSE TO MARY'S VISIT (vv. 39-44)

    A. The visit occurs in Judea, the Southern kingdom.

    B. Elizabeth was filled with the Holy Spirit.

       1. A physical reaction

       2. A spiritual reaction

       3. An intellectual reaction

       4. A recognition of true belief

III.   MARY'S SONG (vv. 46-56)

    A. A song glorifies the Lord. (1 Corinthians 10:31)

    B. True worship

       1. Includes rejoicing (v. 47)

       2. Experienced by the humble (v. 48)

       3. True greatness is seen when God is at work. (vv. 48-19)

       4. Recognizes God's mercy (vv. 50-51)

       5. Recognizes God at work (vv. 51-52)

       6. Knows that we cannot be proud and humble at the same time (vv. 51-52)

       7. Indicated by a hunger for God (v. 53)

IV.   THE BIRTH OF JOHN THE BAPTIST (vv. 57-66)

    A. Believers can share each other's joy. (vv. 57-58; See the book of Philippians for a study of joy.)

    B. The forerunner's name would be John. (vv. 59-63)

       1. We must choose God's word over what others say, even our relatives.

       2. Spouses should always work together as one in the Lord. (v. 63)

    C. "Unbelief made Zechariah mute; faith opened his lips." (vv. 20, 64)

    D. This story really was "breaking news." (vv. 65-66)

V.   ZECHARIAH'S SONG (vv. 67-79)

    A. Believers filled with the Holy Spirit will have a song. (v. 67)

    B. Elements of worship

        1. Praise (v. 68)

        2. Redemption (v. 68)

        3. Salvation (v. 69)

          a. From our enemy

          b. From those who hate us (vv. 71, 74)

        4. Mercy (v. 72)

        5. Remembrance of what God has said (vv. 72-73)

        6. Serving God in holiness & righteousness (v. 75)

        7. Leads us to prepare others for the Lord (v. 76)

          a. Sharing the salvation message (v. 77)

          b. Sharing how our sins may be forgiven (v. 77)

          c. Sharing how we know all this (v. 78)

          d. Sharing the message of light, peace, and victory over death

VI.   JOHN'S BIOGRAPHY (v. 80)

    A. He grew.

    B. He developed spiritually.

    C. He lived in the desert.

Lesson 3

"The Birth of the Messiah"

Luke 2:1-20

I. JESUS, THE MESSIAH, WAS THE CHILD OF
    PROPHECY.
    A. God identifies the Messiah in the Old Testament.
       1. Isaiah 9:1-7
       2. Isaiah 53:1-12
    B. The Messiah's birthplace foretold in Micah 5:2
    C. The Messiah is identified in the New Testament.
       1. Galatians 4:4-5
       2. John 1:40-42
       3. John 4:25-26

II. JESUS, THE MESSIAH, WAS INTRODUCED BY
    UNUSUAL WAYS, THROUGH VARIOUS PEOPLE,
    TO DIFFERENT PEOPLE.
    A. Mary and Joseph – The creator born like us
    B. By angels to the shepherds (vv. 15-20)
    C. To the Inn Keeper
       1. The keeper: cruel, inhospitable
       2. Why do we have no room for Him?
          a. Minds over crowded: jobs, pleasure
          b. No time to check out this baby
          c. Too busy – preoccupied
          d. Paying no attention to spiritual matters

III. JESUS, THE MESSIAH, IS INTRODUCED TO US BY
     THE HOLY SPIRIT.
     A. Each of us is responsible.

24

B. What is your response to the Messiah?
1. Doing God's will does not guarantee comfort and convenience.
2. Romans 8:28
C. We must never define where God can work.
1. Do we limit God by our expectations?
2. Have we seen where God is at work in our sin darkened world?
3. How did God visit you?
4. Is Jesus only a pretty little baby boy?
5. Have you considered the adult life of Jesus?
   a. Why he was hated?
   b. Why didn't the religious people like Him?
   c. Why did He die?
   d. How did He get out of the grave, and what does it mean?
6. Did you fear what was happening to you when you first experienced the Lord?
   a. Fear?
   b. A deep consciousness of sin?
   c. Other
7. What do you want from the Savior?
   a. Deliverance from:
      i. _____
      ii. _____
      iii. _____
   b. Healing from:
      i. _____
      ii. _____
      iii. _____

c. Assurance of :
   i. _____
   ii. _____
   iii. _____

Lesson 4

"Jesus, the Dividing Line of History"

Luke 2:21-52

I. HIS PRESENTATION IN THE TEMPLE
    A. Dedicated by His parents to God (vv. 21-24)
    B. Confirmed by Anna as the Messiah of Israel (vv. 36-38)
    C. Described as the model child of the world (vv. 39-40)
       1. Growth
       2. Strength
       3. Wisdom
       4. The grace of God
          a. John 1:17
          b. Romans 3:21-26; 5:17

II. HIS MISSION DEFINED BY SIMEON (vv. 25-35)
    A. He declared what the Holy Spirit revealed to him. (vv. 26; 29; 30)
    B. He describes the salvation God gives.
       1. God provided salvation. (v. 31)
       2. Will include the Gentiles (v. 32)
       3. Denotes God's choice of Israel (v. 32)
    C. He is the dividing line of history. (vv. 33-39)
       1. Is destined to cause the falling and rising of many in Israel (v. 34)
       2. Will be the + or - sign regarding people's decisions about life (John 1:10-13)
       3. Our choices about Him will bring (Matthew 10:34-39)

       a. Life or Death

       b. Peace or Sorrow

       c. Togetherness or Divisiveness

D. He is either our Savior or Judge.

    1. Matthew 10:32-33

    2. Luke 16:25-26

    3. John 3:18-21

Lesson 5

"John, the Baptist: The Forerunner of Jesus"

Luke 3:1-20

I.   THE CALLING OF JOHN EXPERIENCED
   A. To announce the coming of Christ, and His presence
   B. To prepare the way of the Lord
      1. To understand God's grace and power to effect a complete change of heart and mind
      2. To make it possible for us to be genuinely converted so that we could receive God's salvation
      3. To make straight His paths
         a. Provide the Lord with a ready access into their hearts and lives.
         b. Be willing to make straight whatever was crooked or "not in line with God's will in your life"
         c. To be willing to clear away all the obstructions in their lives, such as self-righteous and smug complacency
         d. The wilderness through which a path must be made ready for the Lord is in the final analysis: the people's hearts. (The human heart, by nature, is inclined to do evil. See Jeremiah 17:9.)
         e. Perverse and deceitful habits must be broken.
   C. The very sight of the actual wilderness had to show the people that they were spiritually wandering in the desert of their lives.

D. Indifference, unconcern, and walking the sinful path must be broken and surrendered to God.

II. THE CONTENT OF JOHN'S MESSAGE
   A. Expected a baptism that was the result of a real conversion
      1. It required a radical change of heart and mind that leads to a complete turnabout of life.
      2. True conversion has the element of a genuine sorrow that turns us away from all the evil in our lives.
      3. True conversion has the element of turning to the Lord for His work in our lives.
   B. Expected fruit-bearing
   C. Can't depend on our ancestors' faith
   D. Judgement is at hand now, for those without fruit. (John 3:18)
   E. The final judgement of God's wrath is reserved for the future. (2 Thess. 1:8-9)
      1. The final wrath is connected with the second coming of Christ.
      2. No one will escape the judgment without genuine conversion.
      3. There is a way of escape for the truly repentant. (v. 8; Acts 3:19)
   F. To delay is guaranteed tragedy. (2 Corinthians 6:2)
   G. Preachers are effective only when they are true to the word of God and preaching repentance for the forgiveness of sin.

III. THE CONVERSIONS FROM JOHN'S PREACHING (vv. 10-14)
   A. True conversion always implies sorrow for sin and

forsaking the old way of life.

B. What should we do now?

1. Give complete, whole-hearted obedience to what God says do.

2. Our sin is so destructive that it must not be pampered. Deal with it now!

C. The bottom-line is that genuine conversion amounts to showing genuine love. (Note: As an example, see how John answered all 3 questions in vv. 10-14.)

Lesson 6

"How God as a Man Identified with Us"

Luke 3:21-37

I. BY BAPTISM

    A. Baptism is symbolic of the washing away of our sin. (Romans 6:1-7)

    B. Baptism pictures Christ publicly assuming His task.

        1. Dying in the likeness of a sinner

        2. Atoning for sin

        3. Rising to show victory over sin

           a. Death

           b. Burial

           c. Resurrection

    C. The water of baptism signifies the necessity of being cleansed.

        1. Jesus was sinless.

           a. John 8:46

           b. 2 Corinthians 5:21

           c. Hebrews 4:15

        2. Jesus took on Himself our guilt, and vicariously bore its punishment.

           a. Isaiah 53:5-8, 11-12

           b. Mark 10:45

           c. 2 Corinthians 5:21

           d. Galatians 3:13

        3. To bring about this vicarious redemption, the Holy Spirit descends on Jesus, qualifying Him (in His human nature) for the task of being the Savior from

sin.

     a. Isaiah 11:2

     b. Luke 4:18-19

  4. God spoke to assure approval of the Messiah's task. (v. 22b)

  5. John introduced Jesus the next day as the Savior. (John 1:29-31)

II.   <u>BY PRAYER</u>

  A. Disciples should always pray, and never give up. (Luke 18:1)

  B. The model prayer teaches the principles of prayer. (Matthew 6:5-15)

  C. Prayer begins by asking God for mercy. (Luke 18:9-14)

  D. Jesus is the model of a praying man.

III.   <u>BY RECEIVING THE HOLY SPIRIT</u>

  A. The baptism of the Holy Spirit happens when we are born again. (1 Corinthians 12:13)

  B. The Holy Spirit takes our weakness, and even intercedes for us according to God's will. (Romans 8:26-27)

  C. The believer cannot witness apart from the Holy Spirit's power. (Acts 1:8)

IV.   <u>BY GOD'S TESTIMONY OF APPROVAL</u>

  A. God's approval (v. 22)

  B. God's word assures of His approval of all who believe in the Son of God.

     1. John 3:16-18

     2. John 3:36

Lesson 7

"The Reality of Temptations"

Luke 4:1-13 (Part 1)

I.   <u>WHAT IS TEMPTATION?</u>
   A. Definition
      1. To try to make a person do something that is evil, or wrong in the sight of God
      2. To provoke, or entice someone to an immoral or ungodly act
   B. Temptation's purpose is to destroy a person through sin, leading to death and hell.
   C. Temptation's ultimate goal is to lead human beings to worship the Devil rather than God.

II.   <u>WHO DOES THE TEMPTING?</u>
   A. God is never the tempter. (James 1:13)
   B. Satan is the primary tempter, the adversary, the destroyer. (v. 3)
   C. The world system
      1. The religious system
         a. Religion without God
         b. The antichrist vs. Christ, the true Savior and Lord
         c. The Cults vs. the Bible
         d. The Occult vs. the Bible
      2. The government system
         a. Corrupt, deceitful, and untruthful
         b. Double standards, blind to the faith and principles of our founding fathers

3. The pleasure and entertainment industry
   a. Tempting or testing God by living life on the edge
   b. Life without restraints and limits
   c. Movies that are gory, sadistic, sin-filled, loaded with terror, filled with horror, sexually tempting, and glorifying the ugly and evil nature of man
4. The philosophical and educational system of our world
   a. Atheistic - no God
   b. Evolutionary - no creator
   c. Anti-Commandments - no absolute standards
   d. Pro-choice in everything
   e. The belief that no one can tell me what to do. I am accountable to no one.
   f. No authorities over us: Neither God, our parents, the law, nor our teachers (Judges 21:25)
   g. Humanistic
      i. Man is the center of everything.
      ii. Life has no value.
      iii. Marriage is an institution of man, not God.
      iv. No judgment day is coming.
5. We human beings
   a. Tempt one another
   b. Lead them down the dark alleys without light
   c. Drag people to destruction, ending in hell itself

III. <u>WHO IS TEMPTED?</u>
A. The first couple on earth: Eve and Adam
B. Every one of us

C. Beware! No one is exempt. (1 Corinthians 10:1-13)

D. The well-known, and the unknown

E. The rich and the poor

F. The educated and uneducated

G. The children, youth, and adults

H. The young and the old

IV. <u>THE BIBLE PROVES ITSELF OVER AND OVER TO BE THE AUTHENTIC WORD OF GOD. IT PRESENTS THE GOOD AND BAD</u>.

A. Abraham and Isaac – to lie

B. Jacob – to cheat

C. Moses – to murder

D. David – to commit adultery

E. Ahab – to seize power by hook or crook

F. Daniel – to give up on God

G. Peter – to deny the Lord

H. Judas – to betray Jesus

I. Paul – to choose religion over God

J. Solomon – to choose false "gods" over "Yahweh", our Creator, Lord, and God

K. Even Jesus

Lesson 8

"The Reality of Temptations"

Luke 4:1-13 (Part 2)

V. WHAT ARE OUR COMMON TEMPTATIONS?
   A. The three temptations of Jesus in Luke
      1. The first temptation: to entice Jesus to doubt God's care (vv. 3-4)
      2. The second temptation: to entice Jesus to gain kingship of the world by worshipping the Devil. If Jesus yielded, there would be no cross, and no Savior. (vv. 5-8)
      3. The third temptation: to entice Jesus to test God's promise to protect Jesus from physical harm (vv. 9-12)
   B. Our temptations - common to all - are summed up in 1 John 2:15-17.
      1. The cravings of sinful man
         a. Food and water
            i. Psalm 78:18
            ii. Esau
            iii. Jesus
         b. Substances foreign to the body
            i. Alcohol
            ii. Smoking
            iii. Drugs
            iv. Gluttony
         c. Sexual satisfactions
      2. The lust of our eyes

a. Satisfy the five senses

b. Desire for more and more money

c. Gambling: money over a family

    i. Sacrificing necessities by taking chances

    ii. Greed (1 Timothy 6:9)

d. Loving material things above God

e. Sexual temptation starts with the eyes. (Matthew 5:27-28)

3. The boasting of what we have and do

a. A well-known intellect

b. A high-paying job

c. Educational achievement

d. Luxurious houses

e. The swankiest neighborhood in town

f. A position of leadership, command, or power

g. The latest fashions in clothing, cars, recreational equipment

h. Our children or grands

VI.   HOW DOES TEMPTATION TAKE PLACE?

A. Satan attacks our mind, will, and emotions.

1. He tempted Eve out rightly with no warning.

2. He tempted Jesus out rightly: completely, entirely without reservation.

3. He tempted Jesus at His weakest moment, when He was tired, exhausted, weak, thirsty, hungry.

B. The origin of our temptations is attributed to our fallen human nature. (Ephesians 4:22)

VII.   HOW DO WE WIN THE BATTLE OVER TEMPTATIONS?

A. Follow the example of how Jesus defeated Satan.

1. His use of God's word (Luke 4:4, 8, 12)

    2. His commitment to the Father's will: Gethsemane

    3. His resolve to resist the Devil (James 4: 7-10)

B. Watch yourself. (Galatians 6:1)

C. Learn key verses by memory. (1 Corinthians 10:13)

D. Learn pertinent subject texts . (1 Corinthians 6:18-20)

E. Determine that whatever you do will be done for God's glory. (1 Corinthians 10:31)

F. Realize that the body is weaker than the spirit. (Matthew 26:41)

Lesson 9

"Jesus Defines His Task"

Luke 4:14-44

I. HE TAUGHT THE WORD OF GOD. (vv. 14-17)
    A. His Bible was the word of God.
    B. If Jesus taught the Bible as God's word, why should we teach anything else?
    C. Hebrews 4:12-13

II. JESUS ATTENDED THE SYNAGOGUES REGULARLY.
    A. What is the church?
    B. What does His example teach us regarding our excuses for not being a part of the church?

III. HE IDENTIFIED THOSE TO WHOM HE WAS SENT.
    A. The Jews (v. 15)
    B. The Gentiles (vv. 24-27)

IV. HE IDENTIFIED HIMSELF.
    A. As a teacher of God's word (vv. 15-17, 31-32)
       1. He knew the hearts of the people. (vv. 23-24)
       2. He spoke the truth always. (vv. 28-30)
    B. As the Great Physician
       1. To heal the spirit (vv. 33-37)
       2. To heal the bodies (vv. 38-39)
       3. To heal the whole person (v. 40)
    C. As a preacher of the Word of God (vv. 43-44)

V. HE DESCRIBED HIS MISSION AS THE MESSIAH. (vv. 18-19)
    A. As anointed to preach good news to the poor

1. 1 Corinthians 1:26-31
2. Matthew 5:3 – "poor in spirit"
3. The truly poor people of our world have nothing material-wise.
4. Their only hope is the kingdom of God.

B. To proclaim freedom for the prisoners
   1. Those in occupied countries
   2. Those serving time as prisoners for real crimes
   3. Those in the bondage of sin
      a. _____
      b. _____
      c. _____
      d. _____
      e. _____
      f. _____
      g. _____

C. To give recovery of sight to the blind
   1. John 9:25
   2. John 9:39-41

D. To release the oppressed
   1. Those mentally and emotionally sick
   2. Those bound by worry, anxiety, depression
   3. Those who live in troubled families
   4. Those in bondage
      a. Who endure godless philosophies
      b. Who live under a tyrant's rule
      c. Who risk their lives by standing up to the evil rulers and beliefs opposed to the Bible

E. To proclaim the year of the Lord's favor (v. 19)

Lesson 10

"The Calling of Jesus' Disciples"

Luke 5:1-11

I. JESUS' REVELATION OF THEIR MINISTRY
   A. Jesus did what God sent Him to do. (vv. 1-4)
   B. Almost any place was His pulpit.
      1. A boat; a synagogue; a mountain; a crowded house
      2. What's the lesson for us?
      3. How big should the preacher's audience be?
      4. What's the answer to what Jesus commands or asks of us?
   C. The Lord sent them to a certain place to fish.
      1. An example of Lordship
      2. Was there anything He did not know?

II. JESUS' REWARD FOR OBEDIENCE
   A. Peter was reluctant to obey.
      1. Jesus was only a carpenter.
      2. Why did Peter decide to obey?
   B. Meaning of the large catch of fish (Scriptures: God's provision is abundant.)
   C. The multiplying effect
      1. In one year 50 disciples make 1 each = 100
      2. Two years 100 disciples make 100 = 200
   D. Obedience leads us from knowing Jesus as Savior to Lord. (v. 8)
   E. Obedience teaches that the Lord cares about small things.
   F. Obedience to Jesus leads to seeing Jesus as Lord and

ourselves as poor, undeserving sinners. (v. 8)

III.   JESUS' REVELATION TO THEM OF A GREATER MARKET

    A. Jesus showed them a great school of fish.

    B. The school of fish taught them the real need: catch people, more important than any catch of fish.

    C. The principles of catching people

        1. Be filled with the Holy Spirit. (Ephesians 5:18)

        2. Pray.

        3. Depend on the Holy Spirit.

        4. Radiate the love of God all day, every day.

    D. The methods of catching people

        1. Go where people are.

        2. Talk with anyone of any race or people group.

        3. Talk with anyone who will listen.

        4. Listen to anyone's story.

        5. Do not pre-judge anyone.

        6. Speak their language.

        7. Ask questions.

        8. Answer their questions.

        9. Be truthful, but positive.

        10. Do not compromise the truth.

    E. Seeing Jesus as Lord leads to eagerness in following Him in radical discipleship.

        1. Their past is behind them.

        2. Their future is committed to Jesus one day at a time.

Lesson 11

"Jesus: The Holistic Doctor"

Luke 5:12-16

I. THE HEALER AND THE DISEASE
   A. Leprosy: like "cancer"; no cure; contagious; compare with A.I.D.S
   B. The leper: untouchable; advanced stage; hopeless
   C. The healer: instant and complete healing
      1. By God's power
      2. Touched by what hurts us

II. THE HEALED AND THE CURE
   A. People needed Him.
   B. The healed needed to show their faith.
   C. The leper got close to Jesus.
      1. Wasn't afraid of the doctor
      2. Had to go on his own or be taken to the doctor

III. THE HEALED AND THE RESULTS
   A. Jesus' healing required no rechecks.
   B. Jesus often gave orders to the healed.
   C. The order:
      1. Show yourself to the Priest.
      2. Why? To restore contact with people.
   D. Lessons for us:
      1. We must be seen as evidences of our healing; of our salvation; seeing is believing; often.
      2. Healings brought people to Jesus.
         a. To hear Him
         b. To be healed by Him

IV.   THE HEALER'S CHARACTERISTICS
    A. Never presumed on God's power
        1. Was the Son of God, but worked as a man
        2. Miracles pointed to God, not Himself.
        3. His strength came from prayer and faith in God.
    B. Our Great Physician lives forever.
        1. Never dies
        2. Never closes His practice
        3. Open at all hours
        4. Sees anyone who desires to see Him
        5. No insurance required
        6. Takes time with every patient
        7. Sometimes He heals our physical conditions, but He ultimately heals all who come to Him – Heaven.
        8. What would you do if you had no hope forever?

Lesson 12

"The 4-H Club Story of the Bible"

Luke 5:17-26

I.   <u>THE HELPLESS</u>

     A. A paralytic

     B. Little children (Matthew 19:14)

     C. Orphans and widows (James 1:27)

     D. Various needs, illnesses, situations, sins

     E. Spiritually lost people (Luke 19:10)

II.   <u>THE HINDERERS</u>

     A. Religious Jews; why present?

     B. The press corps

     C. The rubberneckers

     D. Types of people who hinder:

        1. Get excitement from tragedy

        2. Want to say they were there

        3. Want to see a miracle

     E. Satan, for sure

III.   <u>THE HELPERS</u>

     A. The four men in the story

     B. Who are Christian helpers?

        1. Those who see a need

        2. Those who unite faith and good works (James 2:14-17)

        3. Those who get involved (Luke 10:25-37)

           a. The wrong question: Don't ask, "Who is My Neighbor?"

           b. The right question: Ask, "Am I a Neighbor?"

        4. Those who pay the price to follow Christ

IV.   THE HEALER: JESUS, THE SAVIOR AND LORD
     A. Jesus: teacher, preacher, and healer
     B. He saw people on the inside.
     C. He saw the greatest need of any person. (v. 20)
     D. He saw the whole person.

Lesson 13

"What's Up with Jesus and Sinners?"

Luke 5:27-32

I. INTRODUCTION
  A. He's on the up and up.
  B. Sales are up.
  C. She's looking up in her health problems.
  D. The stock market is…
  E. He's up on his…
  F. Elijah went up to…
  G. Jesus "was taken up before their very eyes."

II. JESUS IS UP TO SEEKING SINNERS
  A. Levi, a crooked tax collector (vv. 27-28)
    1. A hated group
    2. Tariffs and crookedness
    3. Jesus' impact on him
  B. All types of "sinners" (vv. 29-30)
  C. The "sick"; not the healthy – spiritually speaking
  D. Sinners, not the righteous
  E. The riffraff, the scum of the earth
  F. The lost, straying, beggars, hungry and thirsty, the burdened ones
  G. The prostitute mother
  H. The druggies
  I. The immoral
  J. The pedophile
  K. The abuser
  L. Many others

48

III.   WHY DOES JESUS SEEK SINNERS?
   A. Matthew 1:21
   B. Luke 19:10
   C. To show that He came to heal the body, the mind, and the soul (2 Corinthians 5:17)
   D. To give spiritual life to the spiritually dead (Ephesians 2:1-3)
   E. To show all of us that we are dead without Christ (Romans 3:10-12; 23; 6:23)
      1. Guilty
      2. Enemies

IV.   WHAT HAPPENS TO THOSE WHO ARE FOUND BY JESUS?
   A. How did it make Levi feel? (v. 29)
   B. They want others to know about Jesus.
      1. To be known
      2. To know
   C. They have received:
      1. Abundant life (John 10:10)
      2. Eternal life (John 3:36; 5:24)
   D. They heard encouraging, magnetic, and eternal words from Jesus.
      1. Isaiah 45:22
      2. Isaiah 55:6-7
      3. 2 Corinthians 5:21
      4. 1 Timothy 1:15
      5. Revelation 3:20
      6. Revelation 22:17

Lesson 14

"The Real Savior Makes All Things New"

Luke 5:33-39

I.   THE OLD COVENANT IS FULFILLED IN THE NEW COVENANT.
A. Matthew 26:26-29
B. Hebrews 8:7-10
C. Hebrews 9:1-15

II.   THE OLD SELF IS REPLACED BY THE NEW SELF.
A. New Birth Required (John 3:1-8)
B. New Life Results (2 Corinthians 5:17)

III. RULES AND REGULATIONS REPLACED BY CHRIST'S PRESENCE AND POWER
A. Old Wineskins versus New Wineskins
 1. Old Wineskins represent a wedding of old traditions.
  a. Fasting
  b. Mourning
  c. Sacrifices
  d. Cleansing
  e. Foods
  f. Sanitation
  g. The Sabbath
 2. New Wineskins represent a wedding of new things, all given by God.
  a. Joy and Celebration
  b. Life instead of laws
  c. Holy Spirit-filled living

B. The Old Covenant versus the New Covenant
  1. The Old Covenant celebrates:
     a. Animal sacrifices
     b. Holy Days
     c. Somber greetings
     d. Looking forward to Messiah's coming
  2. The New Covenant celebrates:
     a. The presence of the Lord
     b. Jesus' death, burial, and resurrection
     c. New life
     d. Mercy
     e. Forgiveness
     f. Words of life and beauty
     g. Because Messiah has come
  3. The Old Covenant believer does good works to earn God's approval.
  4. The New Covenant believer follows the Christ in us, because of what He has done, not to win His approval.
  5. The Old Covenant believer works out of obligation.
  6. The New Covenant believer:
     a. Works for God out of love
     b. Worships out of
        i.   Thanksgiving
        ii. Gladness
        iii. Joy
        iv. Peace
  7. The Old Covenant has:
     a. Tons of legalistic rules
     b. Fast days that no one can live up to
  8. The New Covenant believer's life consists of:

    a. Gratitude

    b. Freedom

    c. Spontaneous service to God

9. The Old Covenant legalist is motivated by:

    a. Ceremony and liturgy

    b. Rote prayers

    c. Canned sermons

10. The New Covenant believer is filled with:

    a. Abundant life

    b. Assurance of eternal life

    c. Peace with God

    d. Sermons and worship led and anointed by the Spirit of God

Lesson 15

"Jesus Confronts the Danger of Religion"

Luke 6:1-11

I.   JESUS AND RELIGIOUS RULES
   A. The Pharisees and other Jewish leaders were wolves in sheep's clothing.
   B. The Jewish laws were misapplications of God's holy laws.
   C. The Pharisees said Jesus was guilty of breaking Sabbath-day laws when He put people before laws.
   D. The Pharisees were more concerned about hairsplitting-rules than God's love.
      1. When rules are above needs, the Lord is under the law – not above it.
      2. Jesus refutes the wolves with the word of God.

II. JESUS AND RELIGIOUS RULERS
   A. The Pharisees
      1. Critical
      2. Hypocritical
      3. Trying to trap Jesus in some error
   B. These rulers thought they had all the answers.
      1. Opposed Jesus because He did not fit their system
      2. Buried God's law under mountains of man-made traditions
      3. Jesus knew their hearts.
   C. Why did the average person believe and follow the Pharisees?
   D. Why should the Creator bow to the creature?

E. Why were they blind? Filled with rage against Jesus?

F. Whoever convicted Him of wrong-doing?

  1. What changes did Jesus need to make to fit in?

  2. What were they missing about Him?

G. What leads people to choose Islam, Buddhism, New-Age, Mormonism, Jehovah's Witnesses above the Bible and Jesus?

III. JESUS AND HIS REAL RULE

A. Jesus said He is God, and He is.

B. Matthew 28:18

C. Jesus is King of all kings. (John 18:33-37)

D. The followers of Jesus:

  1. Submit to His Lordship

  2. Deny themselves

  3. Follow Him wherever He leads

  4. Die with Him

E. His real rule is set forth in Isaiah 58:1-14.

F. True Christians can't be wimpy. The days ahead become more difficult for us. (2 Timothy 3:1-5)

G. Did Jesus do good or evil on the Sabbath?

  1. Healed

  2. Transformed lives

  3. Raised the dead

H. The Pharisees

  1. Made religion a burden

  2. Preyed on the poor and needy

  3. Plotted to kill Jesus

I. The word of God is clear about pleasing Jesus. (John 6:28-29)

Lesson 16

"People and their Choices Regarding Jesus"

Luke 6:12-26

I.   THE CALLING OF THE TWELVE APOSTLES (vv. 12-16)
   A. Chosen after a night of prayer
   B. Chosen from the body of disciples
      1. Learners
      2. Followers
      3. Adhered to Christ
   C. Had a special commission
      1. Represent Jesus
      2. Go by His authority
      3. Go into all the world and make disciples
      4. The New Testament fulfilled the old
         a. 12 sons of Jacob
         b. 12 tribes of Israel
         c. 12 apostles of Jesus
   D. Chosen by the Lord – not because of their ability (1 Corinthians 1:26-29)

II. THE CHARACTERISTICS OF DISCIPLES (vv. 17-23)
   A. Came from everywhere: crowds and individuals
   B. Needed this Man: Jesus (vv. 18-19)
      1. Not reports
      2. Not gossip or rumors
   C. Had certain attitudes about themselves
      1. Poor
      2. Hungry

        3. Mourners

    D. Why they wept (Psalm 119:136)

    E. Experienced hatred and persecution because of their connection with Jesus

III.   <u>THE CONDEMNATION OF UNBELIEVERS</u> (vv. 24-26)

    A. Rich and comfortable

        1. Their woes run counter to worldly standards.

        2. Rewards in this life; no treasures laid up in Heaven

    B. Well-fed on earth; hungry for eternity

        1. The rich young ruler (Mark 10:17-23)

        2. The rich man (Luke 16:19-31)

        3. Why do so many give no thought to sin and salvation?

            a. _____

            b. _____

            c. _____

    C. Laughing and fun now, but a change at death

    D. Receiving the world's applause, but not God's approval

    E. Be cautious about all people speaking well of you.

    F. The life of Christ in us shows light to the world's darkness.

IV.   <u>THE CONSOLATION OF DISCIPLES</u>

    A. Comfort with the cheering news of God's forgiving love

    B. Pardon, strength, deliverance, reassurance

    C. Heaven for all eternity

    D. One day, we will see clearly forever.

Lesson 17

"Love for Enemies"

Luke 6:27-36

I. THE CHARACTERISTICS OF A CHRISTIAN'S LOVE
    A. Love your enemies.
    B. Do good to those who hate you.
    C. Bless those who curse you.
    D. Pray for those who mistreat you.
    E. Lend to your enemies without expecting repayment.
    F. Give to those who ask you.
    G. Do not demand the return of that which is taken from you.
    H. Be merciful.

II. THE CHARACTERISTICS OF A NON-CHRISTIAN'S LOVE
    A. The sinner loves those who love them.
    B. The Sinner lends, but expects repayment.
    C. The Sinner does good for his own kind.

III. THE REWARD FROM GOD FOR HIS KIND OF LOVE
    A. It will be a great reward.
    B. It will demonstrate your relationship to the most High.
    C. Applications of Luke 6:27-36
       1. Anything less than this kind of conduct is unworthy of a follower of Jesus.
       2. Jesus was the first to teach mankind to see the neighbor in every human being, to encounter every human being in love. (Parable of the Good Samaritan)

3. Love goes beyond, "not taking revenge," but teaching that when necessary, one should render assistance to his enemy. (See Exodus 23:4-5)
4. There is no demand to approve of one's evil.
5. Some of these applications were obviously not to be taken literally. (John 2:18-22; John 3:4; John 6:51-58)
6. Jesus is condemning the spirit of lovelessness, hatred, yearning for revenge.
7. Verse 30: The asking is probably born of poverty. (Proverbs 19:17)
8. Verse 30 is hard to grasp. We must understand the Hebrew style that a startling statement is made in order to shake people to arouse them from lethargy.
9. Romans 12:19-21 offers the true explanation. Our disposition should ever be that of returning good for evil.
10. The major principle is found in verse 31. Unselfish love proves that we are sons of God (does not make us children of God).
11. Verse 36
    a. Grace is giving that which is not deserved.
    b. Mercy is withholding that which one does deserve.

Lesson 18

"The Lord's Unexcelled Precepts"

Luke 6:37-45

I. WHAT BELIEVERS DEMONSTRATE BY JUDGING
    (vv. 37-40)
    A. Verse 37 – What goes around comes around.
        1. Prejudice judges others; the judged also become
            judges.
        2. Condemnation of others gives the verdict before the
            trial. Withholding judgment discovers truth.
        3. Forgiveness is a God-thing. If we have received it,
            it is more easily granted.
    B. Verse 38 – Our giving determines our receiving.
        1. Money is not the issue, though it can be included.
        2. Giving without expecting return yields very high
            returns.
        3. Try tithing, plus giving, and watch God work.
    C. Verses 39-40 – A blind man cannot lead a blind man –
        a pit awaits both.
        1. A student will not exceed the teacher.
        2. If we listen to our Lord, we can become like Him.
            (Galatians 2:20)
        3. John 8:31-32.
II. WHY BELIEVERS SHOULD NOT JUDGE (vv. 41-42)
    A. Verses 41-42 – Judgment of others is based on our
        own blindness.
        1. We can't see trees for the forest.
        2. Imagine seeing a tiny, tiny chip of wood in

someone else's eye, but failing to see a 2 x 6 board stuck in your own.

3. Desire to find fault with others leads to self-inflicted blindness.

4. Jesus calls the "judge with the plank" a hypocrite.

5. This is not a command to refrain from evaluation of others – v. 42B. (Galatians. 6:1-5)

6. Without some observations of others (assuming we are walking with God), how could we ever lead another to Christ?

B. Verses 43-45 – The Fruit identifies the tree.

1. A diseased tree cannot bear good fruit. A healthy tree cannot bear bad fruit.

2. No one will ever find grapes on a briar bush.

3. What's inside will eventually come out. (Matthew 15:10-20)

Lesson 19

"When Jesus Speaks, Who Listens?"

Luke 6:46-49

I.   INTRODUCTION
  A. Communication – a big problem; a universal problem
  B. We hear, but don't listen.
  C. In regard to Jesus – a matter of life or death

II.   THE SPEAKER: JESUS
  A. Jesus is Lord. (v. 46)
  B. Jesus is the builder of the house (the home). (Psalm 127:1)
  C. Jesus is the right choice for the house, the church, and the nation.
    1. Joshua – a great model
    2. Joshua:
        a. Made the first choice (Joshua 24:14-15)
        b. Put first things first (Mark 12:30)
        c. Weighed the choices, and made the right one (Matthew 16:15-18)
        d. Made a personal decision (Isaiah 55:6-7)
    3. Joshua led his nation to make choice #1 first. (Psalm 33:12)

III. THE HEARER
  A. Hears and acts
  B. Confesses Christ by the Holy Spirit's power (1 Corinthians 12:3)
  C. Receives God's truth about salvation (Romans 10:8-10)

D. Listens carefully

E. Knows that he owes allegiance

F. Declares that Jesus is Lord

G. Is obedient to Jesus

H. Builds his house on the rock

I. Knows the storms are coming

J. Is not overly confident in fair weather

K. Abides by Jesus' teachings (Luke 6:27-42)

L. Understands that there is only one road to follow in life
    – not two

IV. THE DEAF

A. Different kinds of hearers (Matthew 13:13-15)

1. Choose to be deaf

2. Are hypocrites (v. 46)

3. Are careless

4. Are selective hearers

5. Are foolish: faith but no works; no foundation

6. Are deceived: "It will never happen to me."

B. Our Lord is heart-broken when people reject Him.

1. Loves unconditionally

2. Gives mercy and grace

3. Invites all to His banquet

4. Gives warnings, but we choose

5. Not His will for anyone to die without Him

Lesson 20

"The Kind of Faith That Jesus Commends"

Luke 7:1-10

I. FAITH RESPONDS TO JESUS.
   A. The Lord draws people to Himself. (John 6:44-45)
   B. The Holy Spirit convicts us of our need for Christ. (John 16:5-11)
   C. The Centurion responded to what he had heard about Jesus. (vv. 1-3)
II. FAITH IS HUMBLE.
   A. (vv. 6-8)
   B. Luke 18:9-14
III. FAITH RECOGNIZES AUTHORITY.
   A. (vv. 1-8)
   B. Peter and Andrew; James and John
IV. FAITH IS RECOGNIZED BY JESUS. (vv. 9-10)
V. THE MEANING AND VALUE OF FAITH IN THE LORD
   A. The Lord teaches us the doctrine of Faith.
      1. Hebrews 11:1 – "Now faith is confidence in what we hope for and assurance about what we do not see."
      2. Romans 1:17 – "For in the gospel the righteousness of God is revealed—a righteousness that is by faith from first to last, just as it is written: 'The righteous will live by faith.'"
      3. Romans 5:1-2 – "Therefore, since we have been justified through faith, we have peace with God

through our Lord Jesus Christ, through whom we have gained access by faith into this grace in which we now stand. And we boast in the hope of the glory of God."

    4. Romans 10:17 – "Consequently, faith comes from hearing the message, and the message is heard through the word about Christ."

    5. Ephesians 2:8-9 – "For it is by grace you have been saved, through faith—and this is not from yourselves, it is the gift of God— not by works, so that no one can boast."

B. The Lord sees the evidence of real faith.

    1. Matthew 9:2 – "Some men brought to him a paralyzed man, lying on a mat. When Jesus saw their faith, he said to the man, 'Take heart, son; your sins are forgiven.'"

    2. Matthew 9:22 – "Jesus turned and saw her. 'Take heart, daughter,' he said, 'your faith has healed you.' And the woman was healed at that moment."

    3. Matthew 15:28 – "Then Jesus said to her, 'Woman, you have great faith! Your request is granted.' And her daughter was healed at that moment."

C. The Lord warns of the loss of faith in the end times.

    1. I Timothy 4:1 – "The Spirit clearly says that in later times some will abandon the faith and follow deceiving spirits and things taught by demons."

    2. Luke 18:8B – "However, when the Son of man comes, will he find faith on the earth?"

D. The Lord shows us how to fight our spiritual battles. Ephesians 6:16 – "In addition to all this, take up the shield of faith, with which you can extinguish all the flaming arrows of the evil one."

Lesson 21

"Various Lessons of Eternal Value"

Luke 7:11-35

I.   JESUS RAISES A WIDOW'S SON. (vv. 11-17)
    A. Jesus was always in ministry.
       1. He and a large crowd entered the city of Nain.
       2. He sees a need and takes action.
    B. The miracle
       1. He raises to life the son of a widow.
       2. It began when his heart got involved.
       3. The miracle: a touch and a command
    C. The results of the miracle.
       1. The people were filled with awe.
       2. The people praised God.
       3. Some saw Jesus as a prophet.
       4. Some saw Him as God.
       5. The news spread all around. (Luke 2:10)
       6. A believer in Jesus has no option except to be a witness. (Acts 5:29-32)

II.   LESSONS LEARNED FROM JESUS AND JOHN THE BAPTIST (vv. 18-35)
    A. John expresses honest doubt regarding who Jesus is. (vv. 18-20)
    B. Jesus responds to John's doubt. (vv. 21-28)
       1. Jesus answers by listing the things He has done and taught. (vv. 21-23)
       2. Jesus responds by describing the authentic Godliness of John the Baptist. (vv. 24-28)

3. Jesus' response is seen through WHAT HE DOES and His affirmation of whom we should be.

III. JESUS JUDGES BETWEEN HEARERS AND HEARERS/LISTENERS. (vv. 29-35)

A. The common people (the regular sinners) heard, listened, and responded in faith in God. (v. 29)

B. The Pharisees and Scribes chose to reject God's purposes. Did they reject Jesus?

C. Who are you? Check one.
   1. A hearer only _____
   2. A hearer/listener _____

D. Does wisdom characterize your life?

Lesson 22

"The Lesson of the Forgiven Sinner"

Luke 7:36-50

I. INTRODUCTION: Sin
    A. The word "sin" is hardly used today.
    B. It is joked about more than taken seriously.
    C. It is denied.
    D. It is old-fashioned.
    E. Humanistic philosophy has no place for sin.

II. WE SHOULD CHALLENGE THOSE VIEWS OF GOD'S WORD.
    A. The world has pleasure in denying sin.
    B. The world is a far better place when we see the truth about sin.

III. UNLIMITED LOVE (vv. 36-38)
    A. Given by a "known" sinner
    B. Thoughts on Unlimited Love
        1. _____
        2. _____
        3. _____

IV. UNNECESSARY CRITICISM (v. 39)

V. UNSURPASSED INSIGHT (vv. 40-50)
    A. The master teacher
    B. The only one ever without sin
    C. When Jesus talks, we must listen. Stop – Look – and Listen.
    D. Jesus often taught by parables.
        1. All of us owe a debt to God that we cannot pay.

      a. vv. 41-42

      b. Romans 3:10, 23; 6:23

  2. God forgives big debts as easily as little ones, <u>500</u> or <u>50</u>.

  3. The woman loved because her sin was forgiven.

  4. The unforgiven Pharisee saw no need to love.

      a. Why should he wash Jesus' feet?

      b. Why love so lavishly as this woman?

         i. People would gossip.

         ii. No need to be humiliated.

         iii. Wasn't she going too far?

      c. Why should I be like this woman?

         i. "I'm as good as Jesus."

         ii. "I've committed little sins, nothing major."

      d. No way Jesus should compare me with this woman!

      e. Everybody "knows" this woman.

E. Our Question: What's the real point that Jesus is making?

  1. The Pharisee was not forgiven, because there was no love to indicate forgiveness.

  2. The Pharisee didn't know who Jesus was.

      a. How could He do all these miracles if He was not God?

      b. Where did He get His wisdom?

      c. Could He possibly be our long-awaited Messiah?

  3. The Pharisee was deceived in thinking He had no sin.

F. A Short Survey of Sin

  1. 1 John 3:4 – "Everyone who sins breaks the law; in

fact, sin is lawlessness."

2. 1 John 3:8 – "He who does what is sinful is of the Devil, because the Devil has been sinning from the beginning. The reason the Son of God appeared was to destroy the Devil's work."

4. 1 John 5:17 – "All wrongdoing is sin…"

5. 1 John 1:8 – "if we claim to be without sin, we deceive ourselves and the truth is not in us."

6. Luke 7:34 – Jesus was called "a friend of tax collectors and sinners".

7. Other Scriptures:
   a. Proverbs 14:9
   b. Proverbs 14:34
   c. John 16:7-11
   d. Romans 5:8

G. Statements that Contradict Common Beliefs
   1. It takes more than religion to be saved.
   2. All religious roads do not lead to God.
   3. A person is saved by grace through repentance and faith in Jesus' death, burial, and resurrection.

Lesson 23

"The Parable of the Sower/Soils"

Luke 8:1-15

I.   <u>A DESCRIPTION OF JESUS' METHOD</u> (vv. 1-3)
      A. Going all about, preaching the gospel
      B. His team

II.   <u>THE PARABLE ITSELF</u> (vv. 4-8)
      A. "Parable" – an earthly story with a heavenly meaning
      B. Grain, sown by hand, but landed in different soils
         1. On the beaten path: hardened by traffic
         2. On thin soil, on layers of rock
         3. On thorny soil, choked by weeds
         4. On good soil, rich and fertile

III.   <u>THE PURPOSE OF PARABLES</u> (vv. 9-10)
      A. A mystery – to the listener
         1. A truth unknown except by God's revelation
         2. A truth revealed to those who listen
      B. A mystery to the spiritually deaf
         1. Those who hardened their hearts to the truth; who were hostile to Jesus; who refused to believe
         2. God darkens the heart that refuses to hearken; hardens those who harden themselves.

IV.   <u>THE PARABLE EXPLAINED</u> (vv. 11-15)
      Central Thought: The result of the hearing of the gospel depends on the condition of the heart.
      A. Unresponsive Hearts (v. 12)
         1. React negatively to the messenger
            a. Have a spirit of indifference

      b. Don't want to be inconvenienced (Ezekiel
         33:30-32)
   2. The Devil works in useless things.
B. Impulsive hearts (v. 13)
   1. Superficial emotions; no deep-seated convictions;
      no root
   2. No thought before a decision
   3. Short-lived emotions are validated by the endurance
      of testing. (1 John 2:19)
C. Preoccupied hearts (v. 14)
   1. Early on, some interest is shown, but it soon wears
      off.
   2. Other matters begin to crowd out convictions.
   3. Life's worries:
      a. Eat our souls little by little
      b. Break down resistance and shorten life
      c. Destroy concentration on God: "can't worry
         and pray at same time"
   4. Riches.
      a. 1 Timothy 6:10; Matthew 6:24
      b. A treasure for earth
      c. Material things
         Rate its influence from good to bad:
     Very Little   to   Very Great
     1,   2,   3,   4,   5, 6,   7,   8,   9,   10
                (circle one)
   5. Pleasures of Life
      a. Wrong in themselves:
         i. sexual vice
         ii. alcohol
         iii. drugs

        iv. gambling
        v.   sports (in over-indulgence)
     b. Like a spreading cancer – eating the good cells
D. Responsive hearts (v. 15)
    1. Receive message with open minds (Psalm 119:18)
    2. Hear – Listen – Respond – Cling
    3. Produce great fruit (Galatians 5:22-26)
    4. Contrast worldly values with eternal values

Lesson 24

"Light, Family, and Faith"

Luke 8:16-25

I. LIGHT THAT INCREASES INFLUENCE (vv. 16-18)
    A. A light is made to help us see. (John 8:12; Matthew 5:14-16)
    B. A light covered is meant to conceal.
    C. A hidden light reveals the darkness of our lives.
    D. How we respond to God's light gives more light or takes away the light we have.
    E. God, in the end, makes known what we try to hide.
    F. How we listen to God is the key to a life of Godly influence.

II. FAMILIES THAT FORGE UNITY (vv. 19-21)
    A. The world's idea of a family is one of flesh and blood relationships.
    B. The real family of God is one that hears and does the will of God. (John 7:17; Romans 12:1-2; John 19:25-27)
    C. Who created the first family? God.
       1. Who creates a family of oneness, love, purpose, faith? God.
       2. Who creates a dysfunctional family? The family without God.
    D. Characteristics of a Christian family (2 Corinthians 6:14-18)
       1. Yoke believers with believers
       2. Unite light with light

      3. Live separate lives from the world

      4. Righteousness and wickedness have nothing in common.

      5. The family is the temple of God.

      6. Families of God can change the world.

III.   FAITH THAT VANISHES FEAR (vv. 22-25)

    A. True faith walks/spends time with Jesus. (v. 22)

    B. God is always near when He sometimes seems far away. (v. 23)

    C. Events appear uncontrollable when God is not in the equation. (vv. 23-24)

    D. When fear prevails, God wants us to pray. (v. 24)

    E. God is in control.

    F. God is amazed at their lack of faith. (v. 25)

    G. When we really decide who God is, our fear vanishes.

Lesson 25

"The Divine Physician Meets a Devilish Man"

Luke 8:26-39

I.   THE MEETING: REGION OF THE GERASENES (GADARENES)

II.   JESUS MEETS A DEMON-POSSESSED MAN.

    A. His home: a cemetery

    B. His physical and mental and emotional condition:

        1. No connections; no home; very sad

        2. Demonic sickness; chains don't have to be prisons; had no social relationships

III. JESUS ASKED HIM HIS NAME.

    A. His answer: Legion (6000 soldiers)

        1. A somber personality

        2. Your name

            a. _____

            b. _____

            c. _____

            d. _____

            e. _____

            f. _____

    B. The demons didn't want a confrontation with Jesus.

        1. What they knew; what they requested

        2. The demons are the Devil's Assistants.

        3. Are they still here with us?

        4. Many failures of people can't be seen.

        5. The demons work in the mind and emotions.

IV.   DESCRIBING THIS AMAZING EVENT
      A. The onlookers could not keep quiet.
          1. Nov. 22, 1963 – Kennedy's assassination
          2. Dec. 7, 1941 – Pearl Harbor
          3. Sept. 11, 2001 – The Islamic terrorists' attack
      B. In Luke 8:26-39, the townspeople were angry. Why?
          (Hint: Values)
V.   WHAT HAPPENED TO THIS MAN?
      A. The Demons were gone.
      B. The changes made:
          1. Sat at Jesus' feet
          2. Had calmness
          3. In his right mind
          4. Peace in his soul
      C. Why were the people afraid about this event?
VI.   A REAL HEALING
      A. He came to know the Lord.
      B. Before Christ, he feared; he rejected others. Because
          Christ didn't matter, people didn't matter.
      C. After Christ, the man knew that Jesus was his Lord.
VII. WHAT HAPPENED TO JESUS? (vv. 34-37)
VIII. WHY DO SO MANY RESIST HIM?
      A. Why don't we want godly things in our life?
      B. Why choose the bad over the good?
      C. What can these habits; thoughts; choices; patterns of
          life do for us?
          1. Resisting authority
          2. Disobedience to parents
          3. Drinking alcohol; using drugs; gambling; cursing;
              sexually immoral; abuse; gangs; hatred and bad
              attitudes; lazy; sadistic; boring; failures; abuse;

hypocrisy; lying; unbelieving; denying GOD'S truth and love

D. Do you now see why the church should be a house for sinners?

IX. <u>WHO IS BEHIND ALL THIS EVIL, BRAINWASHING, AND CORRUPTION IN OUR WORLD</u>?

A. John 8:42-47

B. The Devil, a liar, killer, stealer, destroyer, deceiver, the great red dragon in a $900 suit and tie of Wall Street.

X. <u>WHO IS THE ONE WHO CAN TRULY REVEAL AND DESTROY THE EVIL ONE</u>?

A. Matthew 1:21

B. John 14:6

C. John 10:27-30

D. John 3:16-18

E. John 3:36

F. John 10:10

G. John 11:25-26

XI. <u>JESUS HAD A PLAN FOR THE MAN</u>. (Luke 8:38-39)

Lesson 26

"Sickness and Death in the Presence of Jesus"

Luke 8:40-56

I. A WOMAN WITH AN INCURABLE SICKNESS (vv. 43-48)

    A. A bleeding problem

    B. She touched Jesus.

        1. Healing was instant.

        2. Why did Jesus not know who touched Him?

    C. Her feelings, her faith, her peace

    D. God is the only one who can heal.

    E. Our illnesses

        1. Body; mind; emotions

        2. Broken relationships; hatred; lack of self-esteem; fear; hopelessness; arrogance; loneliness; boredom; inability to believe (or is it refusal?)

II. A MAN WITH A DYING DAUGHTER (vv. 40-42, 49-56)

    A. Jairus

        1. A believer in Christ

        2. His desire

    B. Jesus' response

        1. Knows our motives; often-times, gives more than we ask; responds by His timing (vv. 49-50)

        2. Gives unconditionally; He chooses (John 11:21-22)

        3. Gives instructions

           a. Don't fear.

           b. Believe.

4. Takes action
    a. Goes where the need is
    b. In no hurry
    c. Takes five people
5. Responds to their response to suffering and death: weeping and mourning
6. Crying? What about it?
7. Sees things differently (v. 52)
    a. They laughed at Him. (ignorance)
    b. Death was sleep. (Is there anything that God cannot do?)
8. Performs a miracle (gives her spirit back)
C. Our response to the story
    1. Can Jesus do anything with us after we die?
    2. What are we doing about the spiritually dead (alive in the flesh) all around us? (Ephesians 2:1-9)

Lesson 27

"The Mission of Jesus Through Disciples"

Luke 9:1-9

I. THE MASTER OF THE MISSION
    A. Jesus, the Lord and Saviour
    B. Jesus, the Supreme Commander
        1. Creator, Lord, Saviour, Judge, Mighty God, Everlasting Father, Prince of Peace, Wonderful Counselor
        2. The force (power) behind the Mission (v. 1)

II. THE MEN OF THE MISSION
    A. The 12 Apostles – ordinary men (1 Corinthians 1:26-31)
    B. Chosen by Jesus, for a mission – no other reason
    C. Responded without question

III. THE MISSION
    A. The 12 had to learn how the Mission could be accomplished.
        1. Jesus: the authority, power behind them
        2. Support; Anyone to lead?
    B. The Lord sent them out.
        1. Not a club
        2. Had to leave their comfort and go everywhere – anywhere
        3. We cannot choose places, or people.
    C. The Lord outlined their mission.
        1. Drive out demons; cure diseases; heal the sick.
        2. Preach the Kingdom of God. (Acts 1:8)

D. They were to depend on Jesus for their needs.
1. Find people. (v. 4)
2. Not waste time on those who rejected them (v. 5)
3. Urgent mission
4. Needs would be supplied. (Phil. 4:19)
E. Their success
1. Healing; demons cast out; people turning to God
2. A big mission; Herod perplexed; people inquiring about Jesus, comparing Him to great and Godly men
3. We are successful when we point people to Christ and lead them to desire Him.
4. "Glory to God in the highest." (Luke 2:14)

IV.   OUR MANDATE
A. Our orders are clear: start at home; go everywhere; build a force of Master-Minded people. (Matthew 28:18-20; Acts 1:8)
B. The Lord's job description: clear and concise.
1. John 14:23 – _____
2. John 15:16 – _____
3. John 15:26 – _____
4. John 16:33 – _____

Lesson 28

"The Real Source of our Needs"

Luke 9:10-17

I.   INTRODUCTION
     A. Many people have different ideas of what they really need.
     B. What do they think?

II.   WHO SUPPLIES OUR NEEDS?
     A. Jesus is in charge.
     B. Jesus is.
     C. God, only, can supply all our needs. (Phil. 4:19)

III.   WHAT DO WE REALLY NEED?
     A. Things we think we need
     B. We really need to know God and trust Him.
        1. To know God, the Father (John 8:19)
        2. To know the truth of Jesus' teaching (John 7:17)
        3. To know about the after-life (John 11:25-26)
        4. To know the truth (John 8:31-32)
        5. To know that Jesus lives in us (I John 3:24)
        6. To know that we have eternal life (John 3:36) and eternal security (John 10:27-30)
        7. To know that our lives can be changed (2 Corinthians 5:17)
     C. To believe in Jesus (trust in Him, be committed to Him, rely on Him)

IV.   HOW MUST WE RECEIVE WHAT GOD GIVES?
     A. Repent and believe the gospel. (Mark 1:14-15)
     B. Understand the meaning of following Christ. (Luke

9:23-25)

    C. Understand that salvation comes by grace. (Ephesians 2:8-9)

    D. Know that the decision to give ourselves to Christ is our decision. (Matthew 11:28-30)

V. <u>HOW MUST THE RECEIVER OF THEIR NEEDS RESPOND</u>?

    A. Keep in touch with our Lord. (v. 10)

    B. Receive our orders from Jesus. (vv. 13-16)

    C. Decide what to do with what He gives. (v. 17)

    D. Share with others what really satisfies. (v. 17)

        1. Religion never satisfies.

        2. Jesus meets the needs of our: Spirit – Body – Emotions.

        3. People without Christ are: empty, missing something, incomplete, focused on earthly things.

VI. <u>CONCLUSION</u>: Jesus keeps on giving; His love and mercy never run out.

Lesson 29

"The Cost of Discipleship"

Luke 9:18-27

I.   THE DISCIPLE'S CONFESSION (vv. 18-20)

    A. Must identify Jesus

    B. Must be YOUR answer

    C. Must understand YOUR confession

II.   THE DISCIPLE'S CHALLENGE (vv. 21-22)

    A. Must obey always, even without understanding

       1. Keep quiet at times.

       2. Stand strong at other times whatever the opposition.

    B. Follow a man who would suffer much (vv. 22)

    C. To be very unpopular (John 1:10-13)

    D. To be a true disciple, whatever the cost

III.   THE DISCIPLE'S COMMITMENT

    A. Deny self, and take up your cross daily.

    B. Follow Christ regardless; Jim Elliott said, "He is no fool who gives that which he cannot keep, to gain that which he cannot lose."

    C. Which world do you really want?

       1. "Gain this one, lose the next one."

       2. I John 2:15-17

       3. Never be ashamed of Christ.

IV.   CONCLUSION

    A. The kind of disciple Christ is seeking

       1. Those who know who Christ is

       2. Those saved from sin and death

       3. Those who die daily for Him

4. Those looking for the eternal city (Hebrews 11:10)
5. The courageous ones (Acts 5:29)
6. The truth seekers (Jeremiah 5:1)
7. Those fully committed to Him (2 Chronicles 16:9a)
B. Consider the eternal gifts that Christ gives the true disciples.
   1. Eternal life
   2. The city that God has made
   3. The Lord's confession to the Father that He knows us
   4. God's approval of us
   5. The exchanged life: The Lord exchanges His kind of life for us who are willing to give up our kind of life for Him.

Lesson 30

"The Transfiguration of Jesus: A Foretaste of our Transformation"

Luke 9:28-36

I. <u>JESUS HAD HIS OWN REASONS FOR REVEALING SOME THINGS TO CROWDS AND OTHER THINGS TO A SELECT GROUP</u>.
    A. In this experience, He revealed Himself to Peter, James, and John – only.
    B. Describe your relationship to Jesus.
        1. Do you have one?
        2. How do you cultivate it?
        3. What do you do with Jesus?
        4. How much can you share with Him?
        5. How much can He share with you?

II. <u>PRAYER AND GOD'S WORD: THE TWO MOST IMPORTANT THINGS IN JESUS' LIFE</u>
    A. Prayer to Jesus: Continually; Special places; Set aside times
    B. Prayer initiated divine action.
    C. When He prayed, He heard from God.
    D. Prayer linked heaven to earth.
        1. Why Moses and Elijah?
        2. The heavenly disciples linked eternity to earth.
    E. Earthly disciples need this story to overcome fear and see eternal things. (2 Corinthians 4:16-18)
        1. The end of earth is not the end of life.
        2. Some prophecy teachers believe that we are the terminal generation.

3. Do we really think that God is surprised by what's happening today?
4. Do we really think that God will allow Satan to have the last word?
5. Jesus told Satan! (Matthew 4:4)

III. THE MESSAGE OF THE KINGDOM OF GOD HAS MORE THAN THE NATURAL EYE CAN SEE.

A. Moses and Elijah spoke of the Lord's Exodus.
B. Our Exodus will come, for sure.
C. Sometimes, things are fuzzy to us. (v. 33)
D. God gives us help in our weakness. (Hebrews 4:14-16)
E. The most important source of our needed information is God's word, not glorious experiences.
F. God's message about His Son:
1. He is my Son, my chosen one.
2. I am well-pleased with Him.
3. Listen to Him.

Lesson 31

"The Reality of Spiritual Battles"

Luke 9:37-45

I. ASTOUNDING ATTACKS
   A. This boy's attack came from an evil spirit and created:
      1. Sudden screams
      2. Convulsions (seizures) – grand mal; petite mal; epileptic; others
      3. Foaming at the mouth
      4. The demons hardly ever left him.
   B. Uncontrollable anger
   C. A fascination with death
   D. An urge to hurt someone, or even to kill others
   E. A hideous, laughing rage
   F. A determination to get evil
   G. An obsession, addiction, or disorder (drugs, alcohol, smoking, anorexia, bulimia – all demonic)
   H. A zombie stare
   I. Racial obsession
   J. Rebellious spirit
   K. A mean spirit, harmful to any available victim
   L. An unforgiving, grudge-holding attitude
   M. A lust: sex, pornography
   N. A lying spirit

II. ANEMIC REACTIONS (vv. 40-41)
   A. The father couldn't do anything to help the boy.
   B. The disciples couldn't help the boy.
   C. We have an anemic generation of believers today.

1. Results? Witnessing? Disciples? A real revival?
2. Worldly, carnal pulpits!
3. Anemic, compromising, ungodly government in Washington, D.C.
4. Isaiah 59.

III. AMAZING POWER
   A. Jesus said, "Bring the boy to me."
      1. Proverbs 22:6
      2. Acts 1:8
   B. Healing; wholeness; and a Holy Family
   C. Amazed at the greatness of God (v. 43)
      1. Zechariah 4:6
      2. Matthew 16:18
   D. What do we want at church?
      1. Performance of men, or the power of God?
      2. A feel-good sermon, or one that touches the heart of the soul?

IV. AWESOME VICTORY
   A. The crowd marveled. (v. 43)
   B. The crowd marveled, but needed more.
   C. The crowd needed to know the reason Jesus came.
      1. The suffering and death
      2. The burial
      3. The resurrection

V. CONCLUSION: It's your life, your choice, your destiny.

Lesson 32

"Inner and Outer Opposition on the Journey with Christ"

Luke 9:46-56

I.   INNER OPPOSITION (vv. 46-50)
   A. The disciples' argument
      1. Different gifts
      2. Why?
      3. Competitive
      4. Acted like pagans
   B. Were they jealous regarding authority and power?
   C. The true disciple: humble; meek; cares for little ones; seeks no recognition; gives glory to God
   D. Difference between Jesus and the disciples
   E. Do we recognize the little ones?
   F. Jesus showed His love for little ones. (Mark 10:13-16)
   G. Inner opposition is overcome with true humility. (I Peter 5:5-7)

II.   OUTER OPPOSITION (vv. 51-56)
   A. People oppose those determined to do God's work.
      1. We know we must be obedient.
      2. Count on it; we will have opposition.
   B. James' and John's attitude had lots of flaws in it.
      1. Why were they opposed to the man casting out demons?
      2. Bigotry must be condemned.
      3. Philippians 2:3
   C. What will revive our church?
      1. Is there a desire to grow?

2. What is our attitude toward: one of another race; a poor person; one who wears the same clothes every Sunday?
3. Do we resent people who have pennies, only, for the offering?
4. Do we want "known sinners" in our church?
5. Will we accept those Christ would accept?
6. Are there some we avoid at church?
7. Are there unforgiving feelings toward some? What happens?
8. Are we willing to allow someone to return who embarrassed everyone?
9. Do we help people return to God and the church, or do we reject them, and lose them forever?

Lesson 33

"The Serious Cost of Following Christ"

Luke 9:57-62

I.   INTRODUCTION
  A. Jesus was clear in regard to following Him.
  1. No weak, conditional commitment
  2. Scriptures
     a. Matthew 6:33
     b. Matthew 7:21
     c. Matthew 22:37-40
  B. Many followed Christ for the excitement and the miracles.
  C. Had these people heard that discipleship meant serving, self-denial, sacrifice and suffering?

II.   NO RESTRICTIONS (vv. 57-58)
  A. The man's bold statement
  B. Jesus saw the man's heart, and reminded him:
  1. Jesus' home wasn't as secure as foxes and birds' homes.
  2. He would experience rejection.
     a. Judea rejected Jesus. (John 5:18)
     b. Gadara begged Jesus to leave them. (Matthew 8:34)
     c. Samaria refused Jesus lodging. (Luke 9:53)
     d. Jerusalem didn't want Jesus on the earth. (Matthew 27:23)
  C. This man is too-ready to follow Christ.
  D. This man had not counted the cost of following Jesus.

III.   NO RESERVATIONS (vv. 59-60)

    A. Jesus asked this man to follow Him.

    B. The man's request seems reasonable.

    C. Jesus is reminding the man that He is Lord.

    D. The destination of Jesus is the KEY to this would-be follower.

        1. Jerusalem: What if he missed it?

        2. The man was too un-ready.

IV.   NO RETURN (vv. 61-62)

    A. The request seems reasonable.

    B. Jesus knew his heart better than the man did.

        1. Priorities are not in order.

        2. Others can't make the decision.

        3. Could his family change his mind?

    C. The man's heart was divided.

        1. A divided heart is unacceptable.

        2. The desire to return to a life without Christ must be crucified. (Galatians 2:20)

        3. Jesus said, "Remember Lot's wife." (Luke 17:32-33)

        4. We cannot look forward and backward, in regard to Jesus, and do any good.

        4. Did the man realize he was living in a dead society?

        6. The importance of the now moment (2 Corinthians 6:2)

        7. We should follow Paul's example regarding following Christ. (Philippians 3:13-14)

V.   CONCLUSION

    A. Who should be first in our life?

    B. Why should the Lord be first?

    C. Who can better determine what we should be doing

with our lives than Jesus?

D. What is Jesus asking or calling you to do now?

E. Consider what true discipleship could do for us now.

F. A wishy-washy, wimpy person could never be a real soldier in Christ's army.

G. Is this the reason that there isn't much or any victory in your life? The Lord must be <u>MY LORD</u> over all, if I am a real disciple.

Lesson 34

"Jesus Defines Our Mission"

Luke 10:1-24

I.   JESUS APPOINTED PEOPLE TO GO TO OTHERS AS HIS REPRESENTATIVES.
   A. Sent them in teams of two
   B. Instructed them that the harvest was plentiful
   C. Alerted them to
      1. How they might be received (v. 3)
      2. Trust God as they go (v. 4)

II. JESUS INSTRUCTED THEM ON HOW TO RELATE TO OTHERS.
   A. Go as a person of peace.
      1. Some will receive them.
      2. Some will not receive them.
         a. We cannot force Christ on anyone.
         b. We cannot save anyone.
         c. Each one is responsible for his destiny.
   B. Form a support team.
      1. Will reside with some, and receive support
      2. Will develop the base of a church

III. JESUS INSTRUCTED THEM REGARDING THEIR MISSION.
   A. God's Kingdom is in the messenger. (v. 11)
   B. The response of the hearer is URGENT. (v. 12)
   C. Examples of how people respond:
      1. The cities of Korazin, Bethsaida, and Capernaum will be judged harshly. Why?

2. Contrast the cities of Tyre and Sidon with the three cities listed above in "C. 1".

3. Some will respond everywhere the message is shared.

IV. JESUS REVEALS THE PRINCIPLE OF PASSING THE MESSAGE ON FROM GOD TO OTHERS.

A. God to Jesus to others, others, and others (v. 16)

B. The message is clear.

1. How we hear is critical.

2. Whether or not we hear is urgent.

3. Our response determines our eternity – our home forever.

4. The tragedy of all tragedies is not receiving Him.

V. JESUS EXPLAINS THE DYNAMICS OF GOD'S KINGDOM.

A. Even demons are defeated by the message. (v. 17)

B. Our authority comes from the Lord of the message. (vv. 18-19)

C. Receiving Jesus as Savior and Lord gives one membership in the eternal kingdom.

D. The really wise and learned person is the one who has received God's message. (v. 21)

E. The Kingdom of God is known only by revelation from God.

F. Lastly, the Lord reveals who the rich people are, and what's really important.

Lesson 35

"Whose Neighbor Am I?"

Luke 10:25-37

I.   THE LAWYER TESTS JESUS. (v. 25)

II.   A GOOD LISTENER OFTEN ASKS A QUESTION BEFORE HE ANSWERS ONE. (v. 26)

    A. Jesus pointed the Lawyer to the law.

    B. Jesus showed him where the answer is found.

III. THE LAWYER ANSWERS CORRECTLY. (v. 27)

IV. THE LORD SHOWS THAT NO ONE CAN FULFILL THE LAW OF LOVE. (v. 28)

    A. Anyone who kept the whole law could have eternal life.

    B. Paul shows this in:

       1. Romans 3:10, 23

       2. Romans 7:14

    C. We see this and cry out to God for help.

       1. John 3:16

       2. John 3:36

       3. John 7:37

V.   THE LAWYER LOOKED FOR A LOOPHOLE. (v. 29)

    A. Jews excluded Gentiles and Samaritans as neighbors.

    B. The Jews had different views regarding the neighbor.

    C. Jesus knew the Lawyer didn't really know the law.

VI. JESUS TELLS THE LAWYER A PARABLE. (v. 30)

    A. Likely, the victim was a Jew.

    B. The attack happened in dangerous territory.

VII.   THE PRIEST AVOIDED CEREMONIAL
CONTAMINATION. (v. 31)
- A. Had he overlooked Leviticus 19:34; and Micah 6:8?
- B. It's easy to be a Christian at church.

VIII. MATTHEW 9:36. (v. 33)

IX.   TWO DENARII EQUAL TO TWO DAYS WAGE (v. 35)

X.   JESUS NEVER COMPROMISED GOD'S LAWS. (v. 36)
- A. Of the 3 passers-by, who was the real neighbor?
- B. The Lawyer asked the wrong question. Jesus asked the right question.
- C. Jesus often asks us if we are being a real neighbor.

XI.   THE LAWYER DIDN'T EVEN USE THE WORD "SAMARITAN". (v. 37)
- A. This parable has built many hospitals.
- B. The parable removes:
  1. Racial prejudice
  2. Class jealousy
  3. Hatred of enemies
  4. Even wars
- C. The bottom line is? Follow the Samaritan's actions.

XII. SUMMARY
- A. What does the parable teach?
  1. The original question asked how we get eternal life.
  2. The answer:
     a. No one could perfectly fulfill the Law.
     b. The Lawyer knew the answer; he had another motive.
     c. God provided the solution.
        i.   Romans 8:1-4

      ii. Galatians 3:13

     iii. 2 Corinthians 5:21

B. What must we learn from this?

   1. On our own, we can never be a neighbor.

   2. Keeping the law cannot be done without Christ in us.

   3. Without Christ, we will never be a neighbor.

C. Am I a neighbor?

   1. The Samaritan showed God to the victim.

   2. The answer lies within us.

   3. If the Christian life isn't working for us, we may have religion – but not Christ.

Lesson 36

"Who Describes You Best: Martha or Mary?"

Luke 10:38-42

John 12:1-8

I.   INTRODUCTION OF THE TWO SISTERS

    A. Martha

        1. Opened her home to Jesus, but makes a negative assumption (V. 40)

        2. Her concerns: the house; the meal; details

        3. Jesus saw her as: distracted; worried; fretful; angry.

    B. Mary

        1. Famous in the Bible, but wouldn't make the evening news

        2. Spoke only twelve words in the Bible

    C. Which sister do I compare with? Or, whom would God choose for me?

II.   ARE YOU MARTHA?

    A. She was a follower of Christ.

    B. She had a number of problems: anxiety; worry; a troubled mind; a temper.

        1. Is irritability a serious problem?

        2. Two illustrations:

            a. Mother and child in the kitchen

            b. Mother and teen-aged girl

        3. A sharp tongue?

        4. Over worked; neglect of health; tension; frustration; ulcers; headaches

C. Her need: Self-control (Galatians 5)

III.   ARE YOU MARY?

   A. Mary is one in a thousand.

   B. She chose the one thing needful for life: to hear Christ; to fix her eyes on Him; to give Him undivided attention.

     1. She was not lazy; she knew Martha, that she was fastidious; knew that the work had to be done; above all, she knew WHO was coming to dinner.

     2. Her priorities were in order: WHO was she listening to? What did HE know?

       a. Was there ever such a teacher?

       b. How often would God come?

     3. She chose what mattered most:

       a. To know God

       b. To hear humbly

   C. Mary's choice prepared her for the crises of life.

     1. Lazarus died! Who came?

     2. Many people don't need Jesus??

       a. They don't need Him in their prosperity.

       b. The bad things "will never happen to me."

       c. Even when their house is dark

Lesson 37

"The Disciple's Prayer"

Luke 11:1-13

I. THE PARABLE (vv. 5-13)
   A. The lesson from our world:
      1. The request for bread is made.
      2. The friends go back and forth regarding one giving
         and one receiving.
      3. The friend with bread finally grants the request,
         because of the hungry man's persistence.
   B. The Father in heaven generously answers the request –
     no fuss.
      1. The Father – unlike the friend
      2. Perseverance
         a. Ask – believes and expects
         b. Seek – asking; acting on the Word; looks until
            he finds
         c. Knocks – asking; acting; persevering
         d. Note the rising scale of intensity.
         e. The praying disciple never gives up.

II. THE DISCIPLE'S PRAYER (vv. 1-4)
   A. Not the Lord's prayer (see John 17)
   B. Disciples wanted the Lord to teach them to pray: to
     pray; and how to pray.
   C. The subjects of prayer
      1. "Our Father": for believers; not for unbelievers
         (see Romans 8:15-17)
      2. "Hallowed be thy Name." The Christian wants

everyone to know God; recognize His holiness; exalt His name.

3. Our Father is the living God: not an idol; the Name represents the person.

4. "Your kingdom come, and <u>WILL</u> be done on earth as in heaven."
   a. Your rule be established.
   b. Earth become like heaven.
   c. Come into everyone's life.
   d. Replace the Devil's rule in our lives.

5. "Give us our daily bread."
   a. Bread means all that we need.
   b. Not a request for riches
   c. Matthew 4:4; Philippians 4:19

6. "Forgive our sins, as we forgive others."
   a. We cannot receive forgiveness, unless we grant forgiveness.
   b. How can we accept it and not grant it?
      i. Compare our sins against God with others' sins against us.
      ii. Think of the gap between us and God and us and others.
         1.) Me – infinite distance – God
         2.) Me – a step – others

7. "Lead us not into temptation, but deliver us from evil."
   a. I am weak; guide me so that I will not fall into sin.
   b. Help me to recognize Satan's attacks; and to know my strength you give to me. (I John 4:4)

III.   <u>CONCLUSION</u>
    A. God and Prayer: He/His
       1. His answers are sometimes immediate.
       2. His delays are not denials.
       3. He knows best, and sometimes says no.
    B. God is always the BEST FATHER.
       1. He sometimes gives more or better than we ask.
       2. He never lacks anything we need.
       3. He is never bothered when His child approaches
          Him.
       4. He is never taken by surprise, by our circumstances,
          or with our requests.
    C. Midnight never comes with God.

Lesson 38

"Who, Really, Has Control of You?"

Luke 11:14-28

I.   WHO IS BEELZEBUB?
   A. A Philistine god: a man-made god; a false god: means "Lord of the dwelling"
   B. Beelzebub means "Lord of the dung".
   C. The leaders of the Jews were heaping scorn on Jesus.
   D. Whatever his name – he was Satan (or the Devil).
   E. The Jews were saying that Jesus cast out demons by the power of Satan.
   F. He is "Baal" of the Old Testament.

II. APPLICATION AND UNDERSTANDING
   A. Satan will always try to confuse us.
   B. Satan wants to be God, but he is totally evil.
      1. Leads us into temptation, and all kinds of evil
      2. Works in the minds of people, and has control of millions today

III. RELIGION ALWAYS HATES CHRIST AND HIS DISCIPLES
   A. These critics despised Jesus because:
      1. He attracted the drop-outs in society.
      2. The poor, the very sinful, those not welcome in the synagogues loved Jesus.
      3. Jesus claimed to be divine, because He was; He is.
      4. Jesus didn't honor their man-made traditions.
      5. The critics were pious and pompous; Jesus was humble.

6. Critics were hypocritical; Jesus was sincere.
7. Critics were cruel; Jesus had sympathy and empathy.

B. The critics hated Jesus because He healed, changed, gave hope to all people.
1. Critics gave people rules and regulations.
2. Critics led people to believe that they could cast out demons. The blind were leading the blind.
3. The Devil is the "father of liars"; he leads people to oppose truth.
4. Jesus healed this man; now he could speak.
   a. He really cast out demons.
   b. He began to rule inside people.

C. The critics hated Jesus because He bound the strongman (the Devil) and took away the spoils.
1. The Devil flees when Jesus comes.
2. The Devil knows the difference in his kingdom of darkness, and Jesus' kingdom of light.
3. The Devil gave the people:
   a. A false god
   b. Lies instead of truth
   c. No power – only blind submission to his foul leadership
   d. Belief that they could rule their own life; but we cannot without Jesus.
   e. The idea that they could be self-made people
      i. These are always spiritually impotent.
      ii. These believe that each person chooses his way to God, and all roads lead to God.
4. God's Word contradicts the critics.
   a. John 14:6

       b. I Timothy 2:5

D. Jesus is the real Strongman.

    1. He has battled Satan through the ages, and always wins.

    2. The Bible says:

       a. John 15:5

       b. Matthew 11:28-30

       c. Acts 3:19-20

       d. Isaiah 55:1-2; 6-7

       e. Matthew 6:24

E. Jesus says, there can be no neutrality.

    1. In regards to God, no divided heart

    2. Matthew 6:24; 10:37-39

    3. Luke 17:32

F. Jesus will not share His throne.

    1. No half-way Christians

    2. No success in the Christian life

    3. No victory over the forces of evil

    4. A resolution may get rid of one demon, but without Christ on the throne of our heart, the demon returns and brings seven more demons.

G. Choose whom you will serve: Jesus or Satan.

    1. A half-truth isn't truth.

    2. Can't belong to two Armies

    3. A so-called Christian is a traitor if he ever takes the Devil's side.

    4. Not room for Christ and Satan in marriage

    5. A double life brings misery.

H. Now hear this!

    1. Jesus will allow a half-hearted person to walk away from Him.

2. Jesus does allow a person to choose hell as their destination, rather than force a person to follow Him.
3. Jesus knows your heart.

Lesson 39

"What Does It Really Take for God to Get Our Attention?"

Luke 11:29-32 (Part 1)

I. INTRODUCTION
    A. Three things must happen for a person to become a disciple of Jesus Christ.
        1. We must hear about Jesus.
        2. We must hear Jesus.
        3. We must heed (act on, obey) what Jesus says.
    B. When Jesus was on earth
        1. Many heard about Him.
        2. Some made the effort to hear Him.
        3. Few heeded what He commanded!
    C. We will not have real life until we know Him (John 17:3), and obey Him (Luke 6:46).

II. HEARING ABOUT JESUS
    A. Jesus attracted great crowds.
        1. He knew that all who heard did not listen.
        2. He knew His audience: a wicked generation; and "prove it to me" generation.
    B. This audience today has heard about Jesus, but?
        1. Why are you here?
        2. Did you come to hear Him? How does this happen? (Romans 10:14-15)

III. HEARING ABOUT JESUS IS NOT THE SAME AS HEARING HIM.
    A. Jesus told stories that related to people.
        1. About Jonah, the Jewish prophet, and the Ninevites

      a. The Ninevites repented of evil because of one man with one sermon.

      b. The sermon had eight words; and there was no miracle.

      c. Jonah <u>WAS</u> the sign.

2. About the Queen of the South

      a. She will be a witness against Jesus' generation.

      b. She came from far away to hear Solomon: only a man of great wisdom.

      c. Compare the teaching of Solomon with that of Jesus.

      d. The Queen made a journey of 1250 miles; maybe thirty days long.

      e. The Jesus generation had easy access to Him. America, where are we?

B. The people wanted signs.

1. Maybe the word "Jesus" in golden letters across the sky

2. Send Michael, the archangel, to wipe out the Romans

3. Why did they need more than Jesus had done?

      a. Healed the sick

      b. Cast out demons

      c. Raised the dead

4. The <u>rescued Jonah</u>, and the <u>Resurrected Jesus</u> were the signs.

5. Less enlightened people heeded (responded positively) to a reluctant preacher.

6. More enlightened people rejected and refused to heed the Light of the world.

Lesson 40

"What Does It Really Take for God to Get Our Attention?"

Luke 11:29-32 (Part 2)

C. Who Should Have Gotten the Greater Message?
   1. The Queen of the South
      a. A 1250-mile journey
      b. To hear a bright man – lacking in moral standards
      c. No invitation – only reports
   2. The Scribes and Pharisees
      a. Truth in their reach; saw the Son of God
      b. Personal invitations (Matthew 11:28-30)
   3. The Ninevites
      a. Repented at the preaching of a disobedient prophet
      b. Heard an eight-word sermon of judgment
      c. No miracles; no spiritual insights
   4. The Scribes and Pharisees
      a. Heard messages of truth, grace, love and eternal life (Luke 19:10)
      b. What they saw was almost incredible (Luke 4:18-22)
      c. Insights of the Jews
         i.   The history of God's choice
         ii. The laws of God
         iii. The Messiah, a Jew, with them

III. HEEDING THE WORDS OF JESUS
      A. We can run, but not hide from God.

1. Disobedience = disaster
2. Testing will come.
B. We can heed God as the Queen did.
   1. Great effort to hear
   2. Thankful . . . took the message home
C. Jesus calls and wants us to heed.
   1. Knew He was the sign
      a. Miracles were not for show.
      b. Message for the whole world
   2. Spoke of victory for all
      a. Abundant and eternal life for all
      b. Salvation for anyone who desires it
   3. Assured victory for all through His resurrection
D. If we only knew who Jesus really is!
   1. The word of life to encourage us
   2. The truth that we will make right decisions
   3. The light to see things as they really are
   4. The way of life to guide them
   5. The bread of life for the starving
   6. The water of life for the perishing
   7. The Resurrection and the Life to overcome death, the grave, and hell (Isaiah 55:1-3A, 6-7)

Lesson 41

"We Are What We See"

Luke 11:33-36

I. THE PURPOSE OF A LAMP
   A. To banish the darkness
   B. To show what's out there
   C. To show who we are
   D. To reveal the stumbling blocks
   E. To guide us to our destination
   F. John 14:6
   G. To remember "a friend rings the doorbell; a thief comes in the night to break in"

II. THE HUMAN EYE IS COMPARED TO THE LAMP.
   A. The Bad Eye
      1. Is satisfied with the darkness (John 3:19-21)
      2. Can't see clearly and misjudges what he sees; Illustration: "The 20-foot-long deer"
      3. Cannot see the warning signs
   B. The Good Eye
      1. Receives God's gift of the light (John 8:12)
      2. Has the power of discernment (John 2:23-25)

III. THE PERSON IS RESPONSIBLE FOR WHAT THE EYE SEES.
   A. Proverbs 23:7 – "as a man thinks in his heart, so is he."
   B. Isaiah 5:20 – the evil eye reverses the truth.
   C. We must run from temptation. (2 Timothy 2:22)
   D. Romans 12:9
   E. Romans 16:19

IV. THE OPTIONS FOR THE CONTENTS ON THE INSIDE.
   A. We are born with darkness on the inside. (Acts 26:18)
   B. Criminals try to cover the darkness.
   C. On our own, we cannot banish the darkness. We need help.
   D. We see what we want to see.
   E. The sin nature must be recognized. (Romans 3:10; 3:23; 6:23)
   F. We have light on the inside by choice. (Deuteronomy 30:19; Joshua 24:15)
   G. Those who love the Lord hate evil. (Psalm 97:10)
   H. Proverbs 8:13 – fear the Lord . . . hate evil.
   I. Prejudice indicates darkness.
   J. We need the armor of God. (Ephesians 6:10-18)
   K. The importance of scripture memorization

V. CONCLUSION: "Why can't we see the good and choose it?"
   A. Because we haven't been saved from sin.
   B. Because we don't have the Holy Spirit living in us.
   C. Because Jesus is not the Lord of our life.

Lesson 42

"Religion or Christ"

Luke 11:37-54

I. LEADERS OF FALSE RELIGION IDENTIFIED: THE
    PHARISEES: The Pharisees (the separated ones) were a
    religious and political party in Palestine in New Testament
    times, known for insisting that the law of God be observed
    as the scribes interpreted it, especially for keeping the laws
    of tithing and ritual purity.
    A. Were legalistic in regards to keeping the laws on the
       Sabbath, divorce, oaths, the wearing of phylacteries
       and fringes, washing of hands
    B. They kept the letter of the law rather than the spirit of
       the law.
    C. They could not eat in the home of a non-Pharisee.
    D. They were always critical of others, and often looked
       down on "sinners".
    E. They observed the law to the "T", but their hearts were
       far from God.
    F. Their motives were wrong, because they wanted the
       praise of men.
    G. Their evil desires were hidden by their pious show.
    H. Jesus called them hypocrites, because their hearts did
       not match their outward appearance.
    I. They were religious, but made their religion a burden
       for people to follow.

II. LAWS OF RELIGION MADE BY LEGALIST
    LEADERS VERSUS THE CURSES OF JESUS UPON

FALSE PROPHETS

A. Definition of "Woe" – a curse upon; cursed be you
B. The six "Woes" of Jesus:
1. "Woe" to you for tithing to the penny, but neglecting mercy, justice, and love. We can't pick and choose regarding God's law. (v. 42)
2. "Woe" to you because of desiring places of honor, and to be recognized by man. (v. 43)
3. "Woe" to you because your religion is dead, like bones in a grave – no life in it. (v. 44; John 10:10)
4. "Woe" to you because you write unbearable laws for others to keep, but don't lift a finger to help them. (v. 46)
5. "Woe" to you for approving the killing of men of God. Religious people often try to eliminate Christ's followers. (vv. 47-52)
6. "Woe" to you for taking away the key of knowledge from those who trust you with their souls. (v. 52)

III. LESSONS LEARNED FROM THE LORD OF LIFE

A. Jesus will always go when invited. (v. 37)
B. Jesus goes to the heart of the issue without mincing words. (vv. 38-52)
C. We cannot hope to hide our real selves from God, with His infinite knowledge of the heart.
D. False leaders of religion will always oppose true teachers of God's word, using the art of trapping the truth teller. (v. 53)

Lesson 43

"Warnings and Encouragements"

Luke 12:1-12

I.   BE WARNED (vv. 1-3)

    A. About the hypocrisy of false teachers

    B. About your heart deceiving you (Jeremiah 17:9-10; Mark 7:14-21)

    C. About hearing your own words return to you

II.   BE ENCOURAGED

    A. About gaining freedom over fear (vv. 4-7)

       1. Fear not those who have power only to kill us.

       2. Fear God, only.

          a. His power to kill the body

          b. His power to cast into hell

          c. His judgment of sinners

          d. His omnipotence

          e. His omniscience

          f. His omnipresence

          g. His holiness

       3. True fear of God eliminates all other fear.

       4. Why did Jesus so often tell people, "Have no fear," and "Be not afraid"?

    B. About gaining acceptance over condemnation (vv. 8-12)

       1. Confess Him; He confesses you. (Matthew 10:32-33)

       2. Deny Him; He denies you.

       3. Accept Him; have no fear of those who reject you.

4. True belief in Jesus eliminates the tragedy of blasphemy.
5. The meaning of blasphemy (Mark 3:29)
    a. "The act of cursing, slandering, reviling, or showing contempt or lack of reverence for God"
    b. The act of attributing the work of Jesus to an evil spirit
    c. A state of hardness of heart in which one willfully resists God's saving power and grace
6. True assurance
    a. John 3:18
    b. Romans 8:37-39
    c. John 3:36
    d. I John 2:3-6
    e. John 5:24

Lesson 44

"The Parable of the Rich Fool"

Luke 12:13-21

I. LIFE WITH GREED
    A. When "Papa" and "Mama" die, the children show their colors.
    B. The sin of greed can mean the breaking of 9 of the 10 commandments.
    C. All kinds of greed: money-land-property-tools-luxury-using people-covetousness-recognition
    D. Greed is:
        1. Hoarding stuff; stocking up on material things
        2. Worry about what to do with things
        3. Worry about how to keep things secure
        4. Too much concern with personal pronouns: I; my; myself; himself; yourself
        5. Presumption: life for years to come; life for one day; one hour
        6. "I am a self-made man."
        7. No responsibility when "I" have it made
        8. Do what "I" want to do
        9. I deserve a life of complete freedom.

II. LIFE WITHOUT GOD
    A. KEY NOTE: "A man's life does not consist in the abundance of his possessions."
    B. Who made the man rich?
        1. He produced great crops – really?
        2. Was anything ever given to him?

3. Had he ever thought about his parents, grandparents, siblings, slaves, or servants?
4. Did he ever pause to think about air, water, oxygen, where he lived, or the people of influence in his life?
5. Did he know of anyone who loved him?
6. We really can't do anything by ourselves.

C. Who made this man?
1. God
2. Parents
3. A loving wife
4. Caretakers

III. LIFE WITH GOD
A. God called this man a fool.
B. What was missing in his life?
1. God – did he ever even think about the origin of life?
2. Others – a greedy person doesn't need anyone else. *Yes or No*
3. Worship, love, compassion, kindness, caring for others, people, a God-cause worth dying for, a friend whom he could not buy
4. Consideration of the end of life

C. What did he leave behind? *Everything*
D. What did he send ahead?
1. Nothing – wrong answer
2. A wasted life where God was rejected – with a face-to-face meeting with God

E. What can God do for the rich fool? He can give him many things that money cannot buy. The rich fool can:

1. Know God (John 17:3)
2. Have salvation (Acts 4:8-12)
3. Experience forgiveness (Acts 3:19)
4. Live eternally (John 3:36)
5. Be assured of perfect security (John 3:18)
6. Walk in abundant life (John 10:10)
7. Look forward to Heaven (2 Corinthians 5:1-5)

Lesson 45

"The Real Meaning of Worry and Anxiety"

Luke 12:22-34

I.   INTRODUCTION
  - A. This text is for disciples.
  - B. Applies to poor or rich people
  - C. Anxiety: self-consuming thought; emotional torture by opposing feelings; self-control given to someone or something other than God

II.   ANXIETY DEFINED AND DESCRIBED
  - A. Shallow thinking about Foundational Issues
    1. The origin of life and body
    2. The foolishness of security in riches
    3. The danger of seeing this world as home
  - B. God meets our greater and lesser needs.
    1. We must trust Him for the more.
    2. We may trust Him for the less.
  - C. Examples of lesser life can teach us.
    1. Flowers, fowl, and fields teach us.
    2. Lower levels of creation respond without feeling.
    3. God's concern for the birds and flowers means "humans" can trust Him.
  - D. The impotence of anxiety encourages us.
    1. Anxiety works only on our hearts: "mind, will, emotions."
    2. Worry has no effect on the situation.
    3. "If worry could have made me taller as a teenager, I would be 6 feet tall."

E. Material things are the parents of worry.
　1. Greedy people make these their "chief" god.
　2. Who is your parent?
　3. Our "Father" commands us to "Be Not Anxious".
　　a. It is a self-consuming concern.
　　b. It is being torn to pieces.
　　c. It is the opposite of trust in God.

III. ABUNDANT PEACE GIVEN AND RECEIVED
A. God's pleasure is to give us the kingdom. (v. 32)
B. If people should not worry, they should know why they should not.
C. Verses 33-34 teach us the true meaning of material things.
　1. Parting with possessions could bring peace to many people.
　2. Wealth on earth spent to God's glory becomes treasure in heaven.
D. The greatest reason for overcoming worry is faith in a Father God.
　1. He made us; knows our needs; and made fulfillment of them possible.
　2. Worry is a denial of His love and power; trust is the only appropriate response.
E. Seeking and longing for God's kingdom is our greatest need.
　1. Luke 6:38
　2. Matthew 6:33

Lesson 46

"Watching for our Lord's Return"

Luke 12:35-48

I.   THE RETURN OF THE MASTER

     A. The Master is Jesus Christ.

     B. The Lord lived in the flesh for about 33 years.

     C. Jesus is the Master of all who follow Him.

     D. Jesus will come at an unexpected hour. (v. 40)

     E. No one of us knows the day or the hour of His return.

     F. The Lord comes when He is ready; it may seem like a long time to us. (v. 45)

     G. Our "blessed hope" is the return of Jesus Christ to this earth to re-create, and make all things new.

II.   THE REWARDS FOR READINESS

     A. To be ready is to be dressed and prepared for the journey to meet God.

        1. Dressed equals the righteousness of God. (Revelation 19:6-8)

        2. Prepared equals the light of life that shines through us, always pointing the way to God. (John 8:12; Matthew 5:14-16)

     B. The Lord will serve the disciples who are ready. (v. 37 – a time of joy and feasting)

     C. The "ready person" is one who has been a faithful manager while waiting. (vv. 42-43)

     D. Rewards will be given for being ready. (v. 44)

     E. Rewards will be in proportion for the responsibilities given.

III.   THE RESULTS OF DELAYING OUR READINESS

A. The retribution (penalty or judgment) of God is a sure thing.

B. The unready person is judged by the Lord. (vv. 46-47)
1. Is an unbeliever
2. His judgment will be severe for knowing the Master's will, but not being ready to meet the Master.

C. The unready person who does not know His Master's will shall be judged also, but will receive less punishment than the one who knew His will. (v. 48)

D. Those not ready to meet the Lord are the disobedient; the unbelievers; life is a worldly party. (v. 45)
1. I Thessalonians 5:1-11
2. II Thessalonians 1:3-10; 2:5-12

E. The decision regarding belief or unbelief in Christ is the most crucial (decisive, supreme, important) decision you will ever make.

F. Some people delay getting ready for the return of Christ, their death, the end of time, until it is too late.
1. They presume (expect, suppose, take for granted) that they have plenty of time.
2. They have an appointment with death. (Hebrews 9:27)
3. They have left out of their life priority #1.
4. Life is so short and fragile
5. Who knows when the end of life shall come?
6. 2 Corinthians 6:1-2

Lesson 47

"Understanding the Lordship of Christ and Our Time in History"

Luke 12:49-59

I.   A DEEPER UNDERSTANDING OF OUR LORD'S
      MISSION TO EARTH (vv. 49-53)
      A. He came to bring fire on the earth.
          1. Illustration of burning off the woods
              a. The fire burns the underbrush.
              b. The trees are left intact.
              c. This even prevents forest fires.
          2. Illustration of division in the family
              a. Some in the family are true believers. Some are
                  not true believers.
              b. Some practice Christ's teachings. Some are led
                  by the Devil.
              c. Some put tempting things in the house. Some
                  try to avoid temptation.
          3. Light and darkness will collide.
      B. The Lordship of Christ must prevail in the believer's
          life.
          1. There can't be compromise.
          2. Realize your strength. (I John 4:4)
          3. Put on the armor of God; don't ever remove it.
              (Ephesians 6:10-18)
          4. Practice Christ-likeness in thought and action with
              all unbelievers in your household.
      C. The Lord understood His baptism of fire to accomplish
          His mission.

      1. Baptism (Mark 10:35-45)

      2. Gethsemane (Matthew 26:36-46)

II.   <u>A DEEPER PERCEPTION OF OUR TIME IN HISTORY</u> (vv. 54-59)

    A. We are hypocrites who understand weather patterns, but not what's happening in our time. (vv. 54-56)

    B. Why don't we judge for ourselves what is right or wrong; good or bad?

      1. Many can't see the Devil in the details.

      2. The Bible is truth, the best philosophy.

      3. We are being deceived by the Devil's disciples.

    C. Consider the evil views being accepted.

      1. The breakdown of the family

      2. Lying as an accepted way of life

      3. Hidden agendas

      4. Accepting socialism and humanism as our choices over God's word on matters

      5. Spending money we don't have

      6. Applying different rules for lawmakers achieving success at our distress

      7. Choosing abortion over life

      8. Choosing physical habits that cost billions to treat by medicine and psychology

      9. Creating a society that depends on entitlements rather than hard work and ingenuity

      10. On and on and on

Lesson 48

"The Vital Importance of the Doctrine of Repentance"

Luke 13:1-9

I. INTRODUCTION
    A. The teaching/preaching of "repentance" is most essential to Jesus.
    B. The doctrine of "repentance" is absent from most pulpits today. Why?
    C. If revival is going to take place, "repentance" as a doctrine must be placed in the order Christ gave it.
    D. Definition – "a turning away from sin, disobedience, or rebellion, and a turning back to God. A change of mind or a feeling of remorse or regret for past conduct. True repentance is a 'godly sorrow' in the opposite direction. This leads to a fundamental change in a person's relationship to God." (Nelson's Illustrated Bible Dictionary, c. 1986, p. 908)

II. THE DEMAND TO REPENT
    A. Luke 13:3, 5 – "I tell you, no! But unless you repent, you too will all perish. I tell you, no! But unless you repent, you too will all perish."
    B. Matthew 4:17 – "From that time on Jesus began to preach, 'Repent, for the kingdom of heaven has come near.'"
    C. Mark 1:14-15 – "After John was put in prison, Jesus went into Galilee, proclaiming the good news of God. 'The time has come,' he said. 'The kingdom of God has come near. Repent and believe the good news!'"

D. Acts 2:38 – "Peter replied, 'Repent and be baptized, every one of you, in the name of Jesus Christ for the forgiveness of your sins. And you will receive the gift of the Holy Spirit.'"

III.   THE RESULTS OF REPENTANCE

A. Luke 13:6-9 – "Then he told this parable: 'A man had a fig tree growing in his vineyard, and he went to look for fruit on it but did not find any. So he said to the man who took care of the vineyard, "For three years now I've been coming to look for fruit on this fig tree and haven't found any. Cut it down! Why should it use up the soil?" "Sir," the man replied, "leave it alone for one more year, and I'll dig around it and fertilize it. If it bears fruit next year, fine! If not, then cut it down."'"

B. Acts 2:38 – "Peter replied, 'Repent and be baptized, every one of you, in the name of Jesus Christ for the forgiveness of your sins. And you will receive the gift of the Holy Spirit.'"

C. Luke 3:7-14 – "John said to the crowds coming out to be baptized by him, 'You brood of vipers! Who warned you to flee from the coming wrath? Produce fruit in keeping with repentance. And do not begin to say to yourselves, "We have Abraham as our father." For I tell you that out of these stones God can raise up children for Abraham. The ax is already at the root of the trees, and every tree that does not produce good fruit will be cut down and thrown into the fire.' 'What should we do then?' the crowd asked. John answered, 'Anyone who has two shirts should share with the one who has none, and anyone who has food should do the same.' Even tax collectors came to be baptized.

129

'Teacher,' they asked, 'what should we do?' 'Don't collect any more than you are required to,' he told them. Then some soldiers asked him, 'And what should we do?' He replied, 'Don't extort money and don't accuse people falsely—be content with your pay.'"

D. Luke 24:44-49 – "He said to them, 'This is what I told you while I was still with you: Everything must be fulfilled that is written about me in the Law of Moses, the Prophets and the Psalms.' Then he opened their minds so they could understand the Scriptures. He told them, 'This is what is written: The Messiah will suffer and rise from the dead on the third day, and repentance for the forgiveness of sins will be preached in his name to all nations, beginning at Jerusalem. You are witnesses of these things. I am going to send you what my Father has promised; but stay in the city until you have been clothed with power from on high.'"

E. Luke 15:7 – "I tell you that in the same way there will be more rejoicing in heaven over one sinner who repents than over ninety-nine righteous persons who do not need to repent."

F. Acts 3:19 – "Repent, then, and turn to God, so that your sins may be wiped out, that times of refreshing may come from the Lord,"

IV.   THE FAILURE TO REPENT

A. Luke 13:3, 5, 9 – "I tell you, no! But unless you repent, you too will all perish. I tell you, no! But unless you repent, you too will all perish. If it bears fruit next year, fine! If not, then cut it down."

B. Acts 17:29-31 – "Therefore since we are God's

offspring, we should not think that the divine being is like gold or silver or stone—an image made by human design and skill. In the past God overlooked such ignorance, but now he commands all people everywhere to repent. For he has set a day when he will judge the world with justice by the man he has appointed. He has given proof of this to everyone by raising him from the dead."

C. Revelation 2:16 – "Repent therefore! Otherwise, I will soon come to you and will fight against them with the sword of my mouth."

V. THE MERCY OF GOD REGARDING REPENTANCE

A. Luke 13:8-9 – "'Sir,' the man replied, 'leave it alone for one more year, and I'll dig around it and fertilize it. If it bears fruit next year, fine! If not, then cut it down.'"

B. Romans 2:4 – "Or do you show contempt for the riches of his kindness, forbearance and patience, not realizing that God's kindness is intended to lead you to repentance?"

C. 2 Peter 3:8-9 – "But do not forget this one thing, dear friends: With the Lord a day is like a thousand years, and a thousand years are like a day. The Lord is not slow in keeping his promise, as some understand slowness. Instead he is patient with you, not wanting anyone to perish, but everyone to come to repentance."

Lesson 49

"Christ, the Holistic Doctor"

Luke 13:10-17

I. <u>CHRIST AND THE HURTING WOMAN</u> (vv. 10-13)

    A. The event occurred in a synagogue.

    B. Jesus was teaching as He usually did.

    C. A woman whose "bones of her spine were fused into a rigid mass"

    D. A woman: bound for eighteen years; who had to look at the ground always; whose condition always elicited sympathy; who probably felt that she would never be healed

    E. Christ, and His place in our life

       1. He recognized her, and called for her.

       2. He saw her, not as a bother, but an opportunity.

          a. To heal

          b. To save from sin and give her abundant and eternal life

          c. To give joy forever

       3. He saw those whom others overlooked. (Luke 19:10)

       4. He saw her as an individual.

       5. He could release her from Satan's bondage.

       6. He healed immediately.

II. <u>CHRIST AND THE HEARTLESS RULER</u> (vv. 14-16)

    A. The synagogue ruler had a good case of religion.

       1. He believed in the fourth commandment.

       2. He added many rules and regulations to the

commandments.

      3. He thought that man was made for the Sabbath. Jesus said the Sabbath was made for man.

      4. Following the law, truly, frees a person; following the law, legalistically, binds a person.

  B. Christ offers three reasons for what seems to be breaking the law.

      1. Jewish tradition said some work was allowed on the Sabbath. (v. 15)

      2. The worth of human life justified what He did. (v. 16)

         a. A person is worth more than an ox or donkey.

         b. The bondage by Satan was much worse than an ox tied to a rope.

         c. To set this woman free from eighteen years of infirmity was eternally superior to viewing the law legalistically.

      3. Is there any better way to spend the Sabbath than to release one from Satan's bondage?

III.   CHRIST AND THE HAPPY CROWD (v. 13; v. 17)

  A. The woman praised God immediately.

  B. The common people were delighted with all the wonderful things Christ was doing.

  C. Don't real believers get excited and happy when they go to church and see people saved from sin, and delivered from all Satanic bondages?

Lesson 50

"The Kingdom of God"

Luke 13:18-21

I. <u>WHAT IS THE KINGDOM OF GOD LIKE</u>?
   A. The kingdom of God is a place where God reigns.
      1. A place such as the garden of Eden before sin was present
      2. A place "not of this world" (John 18:36)
      3. A future kingdom (Mark 14:25)
      4. A kingdom received at the great judgment (Matthew 25:34)
      5. The Lord will preserve true believers for entrance into this kingdom. (2 Timothy 4:18)
      6. An eternal kingdom (2 Peter 1:11)
   B. The kingdom of God is where God is, and is the rule and reign of God.
      1. The kingdom of God is at hand. (Matthew 4:17)
      2. The kingdom of God is where God's power is at work. (Luke 10:8-9)
      3. The kingdom of God is within you. (Luke 17:21)
      4. The kingdom of God is not a matter of eating and drinking, but of righteousness, peace, and joy in the Holy Spirit. (Romans 14:17)
      5. The kingdom of God must be received as a little child receives it. (Mark 10:15)
      6. The characteristics of kingdom citizens (Matthew 5:1-10)

II.   THE KINGDOM OF GOD IS COMPARED TO A
        MUSTARD SEED.
        A. The mustard seed is a very tiny black seed.
            1. God's kingdom arrives inconspicuously – a child
                receives Christ and impacts the whole family.
            2. God's kingdom starts with one player on the team,
                and grows one by one.
        B. The mustard seed grows into a tree taller than a man,
            and branches out.
            1. The birds nest on the branches.
            2. The kingdom of God branches out to amazing size,
                compared with its beginning.
            3. The method of spreading the gospel by Jesus: 12
                apostles; 120 believers; 3000 believers added one
                day; and on and on
            4. Geographically: Galilee; Jerusalem; Judea;
                Samaria; Egypt; Asia; Europe; etc.
III.   THE KINGDOM OF GOD IS COMPARED TO YEAST.
        A. The yeast causes the bread to rise.
        B. The kingdom message spreads invisibly.
            1. Unseen prayers
            2. Private Bible study
            3. Acts of compassion and kindness
            4. Handing a gospel tract and saying a few words
                about your faith
            5. Small prayer groups
            6. Allowing the Holy Spirit to work inside us
            7. Using codes to share Christ
            8. The quiet witness for Christ that shows by example

Lesson 51

"The Narrow Door"

Luke 13:22-30

I.   THE QUESTION – ARE ONLY A FEW PEOPLE GOING TO BE SAVED? (vv. 22-23)

II. THE DIALOGUE BETWEEN JESUS AND THOSE REJECTED (vv. 24-30)

   A. Entrance to the Kingdom of God will be challenging and difficult.
      1. Entrance to God's Kingdom will be through a narrow door.
      2. Entrance will be one by one, like going through a turnstile.
         a. It will not be a group's decision.
         b. It will not be by majority vote.
         c. It will be an individual's decision.
   B. Many will try to enter, but will not get in. (v.24)
   C. At the judgment, many will find that they missed the deadline. (v. 25)
      1. They plead to get in.
      2. God will tell them that He does not know them.
   D. The rejected will tell God that they ate and drank with Him, and heard His teaching. (v. 26)
   E. God reiterates that He doesn't know them, and calls them evildoers. (v. 27)
   F. The response of the rejected will be sorrow, heart-rending, sadness, and hopelessness. (vv. 28-30)
   G. They will see people from Bible times that they have

read about.

H. People from all over the world will be in the Kingdom.
   1. These chose God's way.
   2. God prepared a grand reception for them.
I. God's order of importance will often be the reverse of ours.

III. THE NECESSARY RESPONSES
   A. The question in verse 23 can't be taken lightly.
   B. The Philippian jailer responded correctly to the question. (Acts 16:29-34)
      1. What must I do to be saved?
      2. He inquired seriously about salvation.
   C. The Word of God gives us the answer.
      1. We must understand that we are sinners. (Romans 3:10, 23)
      2. We must understand what sin does.
         a. Romans 6:23; Ephesians 2:1
         b. John 3:18; I John 3:4; Eccl. 9:18
      3. We must repent of sin.
         a. Mark 1:15; Acts 3:19
         b. We must have deep sorrow for our sin, and desire to turn from it.
      4. We must believe in Jesus: in Him; in His death; His burial; His resurrection.
         a. John 3:16-18; 3:36; 5:24
         b. Romans 10:8-11
      5. The Word of God teaches that salvation is by grace, through faith.
         a. Ephesians 2:8-10
         b. Salvation is free, but very costly.
            i. Free to us

       ii. Very costly to God

6. To be saved is to be born again (John 3:3); to be converted (Matthew 18:2-4); to be transformed (2 Corinthians 5:17).

7. Salvation means a radical change (Luke 9:57-62). It means:

   a. To count the cost

   b. To put Christ first in your heart (nothing comes before Him)

   c. To go with Christ, and never turn back

Lesson 52

"Jesus' Sorrow for Jerusalem"

Luke 13:31-35

I.   THE CAUSES FOR THE SORROW
   A. The Pharisees
      1. Their jealousy, criticism, and rejection of Jesus
      2. Their condemnation of Jesus
      3. Their hatred of Jesus
   B. King Herod
      1. His jealousy of Jesus led to his hatred of Jesus.
      2. His devious and open sins, such as immorality
   C. The people in general
      1. Had rejected Jesus; had desired the wrong kind of Messiah; had refused to understand Him
      2. John 1:10-11

II. THE CURES FOR THE SORROW
   A. If they had only listened to Him, and observed what Jesus did:
      1. Healed people, drove out their demons, and raised the dead
      2. Taught with authority (Matthew 7:28-29)
      3. Offered them real life: abundant and eternal life
   B. If they had only known what His commission was, they would have understood His commitment. (v. 32)
   C. If they had known the price He paid, and would pay, to be their Saviour
   D. If they had received Him into their lives, the sorrow would not have existed.

III.   THE CHALLENGES FROM THE SAVIOUR

    A. I will love you to the end, and die for you. (v. 33)

    B. I have longed, agonized, and sorrowed for your positive response to me.

    C. I have wanted to give you my protection and security. (v. 34)

    D. I have desired to forgive you, but you would not let me.

    E. Your time is running out: your house is desolate. (v. 35)

        1. You may have waited too long, but I'm making a final plea.

        2. You will not see me again until others are praising me for coming in the name of the Lord – to the cross. (Luke 19:38)

Lesson 53

"Humility: The Mark of a True Believer"

Luke 14:1-14

I.   THE DIALOGUE BETWEEN JESUS AND THE
EXPERTS OF JEWISH RELIGION (vv. 1-6)

    A. The setting: Jesus having dinner with a Pharisee

        1. At the Pharisee's house

        2. The Pharisee's deceitful motive: to catch Jesus in a
Sabbath violation

        3. Jesus focuses on a man with dropsy: an abnormal
accumulation of SERIOUS fluid in a connective
tissue or a SERIOUS cavity.

        4. Jesus healed the man.

    B. The Sabbath debate:

        1. Jesus knew their thoughts and challenged the
experts.

        2. The experts remained silent.

        3. The hypocrisy of the experts: they could rescue a
son or an ox, but condemned Jesus for healing.

II.   THE DESIGN OF JESUS' PARABLE (vv. 7-11)

    A. Jesus noted how the guests chose the honored seats,
and told them a parable.

    B. Humility is a freedom from arrogance that grows out
of the recognition that all we have and are comes from
God. Biblical humility is not a belittling of oneself,
but an exalting or praising of God, especially, and
others. True humility does not produce pride, but

gratitude. (Matthew 11:29; Mark 10:45; Philippians 2:5-8)

    C. Humility gives preference to another person.

    D. Everyone who exalts himself will be humbled; he who humbles himself will be exalted.

III.   THE DINNER EXAMPLE (vv. 12-14)

    A. Beware of whom you invite to dinner.

    B. Give to those who can repay you; your reward will be on earth.

    C. Give to those who cannot repay you; your reward will come at the resurrection of the righteous.

    D. Lessons:

       1. How do ushers choose seats of guests at church?

       2. Whom do you sit with at church?

       3. Do we ever say or think, "This is your time to pay."?

       4. Have we ever had a party for the down and outs?

       5. Who sits at your Thanksgiving table?

IV.   CONCLUSION: How can we be more like Jesus?

Lesson 54 Part A

"The Earnest Desire of God: That My House Will Be Filled"

Luke 14:15-24

I.   THE INCOMPARABLE BANQUET OF GOD – PREPARED
   - A. The banquet represents God's plan and purpose for all.
     1. God contacted us – the world. (Isaiah 55:1-3; Matthew 1:18-23; Galatians 4:4-5; Ephesians 2:8-9)
     2. God had a plan, and acted on it – for our salvation. (John 3:16-18; 3:36)
     3. God sent His Holy Spirit to convict and convince the world of our need. (John 16:5-11)
   - B. The banquet is a feast of all feasts.
     1. Becoming God's child (John 1:12-13)
     2. Knowing God (John 17:3)
     3. Receiving eternal and abundant life (John 5;24; 10:10)
     4. Having our sin forgiven (Mark 2:5-12)
     5. Becoming new people: new birth; transformed people; loving people
     6. Having an eternal home with God (John 14:1-6)

II.   THE INVITATION TO THE BANQUET – EXTENDED
   - A. Given by God (v. 17)
   - B. God truly wants us all to come. (Matthew 11:28-30; 2 Peter 3:9)
   - C. God gave the gospel, and ordered believers to share it.

III.   THE INVITATION TO THE BANQUET – REFUSED

A. Trivial (unimportant) excuses were given as reasons.

B. The excuses sound somewhat reasonable.

   1. The farm symbolizes possessions.

      a. The farmer cannot ignore God's laws.

      b. When possessions keep us from God, they own us.

   2. The oxen symbolize making a living.

      a. Work is necessary, but not supreme in our lives.

      b. All work and no worship leaves "Jack" as a lost sinner.

   3. The wife symbolizes homes and families.

      a. The home is the most important institution, but cannot survive without God.

      b. A home without God is like a person without breath.

   4. Nothing fails like success. If we succeed at everything else, and leave God out, we are failures.

C. Excuses we give:

   1. "I got too much religion when I was a child."

   2. "I am too tired when Sunday comes."

   3. "I must be fresh when Monday comes."

   4. "There are too many hypocrites in the church."

   5. "I don't need God." Oh, really?

   6. "Religion is for superstitious people."

   7. "I can't believe in a God whom I can't see."

D. The winds of reality will always overturn our poor lie-shelters.

IV.   THE INVITATION TO THE BANQUET – RECEIVED

A. The pious and pompous religious Jews rejected the invitation with paltry excuses.

B. God invites others, not the religious people only.
C. Our Lord invites all.
    1. The Jews who were rejected by the religious leaders
    2. The well-known sinners
    3. The God-rejecting Gentiles
    4. The crooks, abusers, thieves, killers, adulterers, prostitutes, the proud, the rich, the poor, the young, the aged, the outcasts, all races, all people groups
D. Many did accept the invitation.
E. What led some to receive the invitation?

Lesson 54 Part B

"The Earnest Desire of God: That My House May Be filled"

Luke 14:15-24

V.   THE BANQUET OF GOD RECEIVED BY MANY –
     WHY?
   A. They saw and heard the world's greatest teacher.
      (Matthew 7:28-29)
   B. They saw the Wonderful Counselor; the Mighty God;
      the Everlasting Father; the Prince of Peace. (Isaiah
      9:6)
   C. They saw one who was a man, and more than a man.
      (Philippians 2:5-11)
   D. They saw a man who was sinless. (John 8:46)
   E. They saw a man who was the Saviour. (Luke 2:10-11;
      19:10)
   F. They saw Him die on a cross for the sin of the world, to
      pay the debt for sin.
   G. They saw Him as the risen Saviour.
   H. They saw their need, and repented and believed in
      Him.

VI. THE BANQUET OF GOD REJECTED BY MANY –
     WHY?
   A. They would not believe in Him.
   B. They rejected His Commandments.
   C. They had their minds made up and would not change
      them when they saw the truth.
   D. Why did Herod say no to Christ?
   E. Why did Pilate reject Him?

F. Why did the rich young ruler turn away from Him? (Mark 10:17-22)

G. Why did the Pharisees, Sadducees, and Priests of Israel hate Jesus as they did?

H. Why do people today choose sin, hatred, Godless philosophies – over Jesus?

I. Why would a person give his soul to gain the whole world? (Matthew 16:26)

J. Why do the great majority of people choose evil over good?

K. Do people really believe that there is a heaven and a hell?

L. Do people really believe that God is a God of wrath? (Romans 1:18-32)

M. Death is coming. (Hebrews 9:27) Whose side are you on?

Lesson 55

"The Cost of Being a Disciple of Jesus"

Luke 14:25-35

I. DISCIPLESHIP (DISCIPLE) MEANS LEARNER OR
    PUPIL.
    A. It is a life lived by His authority. (Matthew 10:1)
    B. It is a life of consistent obedience and love for Jesus
       and others.
    C. It includes faith and works. (James 2:14-26)
    D. It is following Jesus without knowing the destination.

II. DISCIPLESHIP IS FOLLOWING JESUS IN OUR TALK
    AND WALK.
    A. No other love compares with our love for Jesus. (v. 26
       – text)
    B. Luke 6:46 – a necessary warning
    C. Disciples cannot be hypocrites.
       1. Matthew (23:13)
       2. Matthew (23:16)
       3. Matthew (23:25)
       4. Matthew (23:33)
    D. Disciples cannot make up their own minds. (1
       Corinthians 2:15-16)
    E. Disciples are unconditional:
       1. In their love for others
       2. In their giving
       3. In their mission
    F. Disciples cannot choose their place of discipleship.

III. DISCIPLESHIP MEANS FOLLOWING JESUS TO THE

END AT ANY COST.

A. Persecution may be expected. (John 15:20)

B. Christians must bless our persecutors. (Romans 12:14)

C. Christians are living sacrifices. (Romans 12:1-2)

D. Jesus predicted His own death. (Matthew 20:17-19)

E. The Lord chooses different directions and endings for His disciples. (John and Peter: John 21:15-23)

F. Tradition says that all of the eleven apostles died by persecution, with the possible exception of John.

Lesson 56

"The Parable of the Lost Sheep"

Luke 15:1-7

I. THE BACKGROUND OF THE PARABLE
    A. Tax-collectors and sinners were gathering around Jesus.
    B. The Pharisees and teachers muttered their criticism of Jesus.
       1. For welcoming sinners
       2. For eating with sinners

II. THE MEANING OF A PARABLE
    A. An earthly story with a heavenly meaning
    B. A God-truth spoken in earthly language
    C. A profound truth that can be understood by a child

III. THE MESSAGE OF THIS PARABLE
    A. A shepherd has a hundred sheep, and loses one.
    B. The shepherd focuses on this one that is lost.
       1. The 99 are safely in the fold.
       2. He searches for the lost one until he finds it.
       3. He personally brings the one sheep back home.
       4. He has a gathering of friends and neighbors to rejoice over the ONE found.
    C. Jesus states that there is a celebration in heaven over ONE sinner who repents more than over 99 who need no repentance.
       1. The 99 are safely in the fold. They have been found.
       2. The ONE lost (unsaved) sinner cannot be left out.

a. Luke 19:10 – the mission of Jesus

b. Matthew 18:14 – not God's will for anyone to perish

c. Examples of Jesus and <u>ONE</u>:

    i. Nicodemus – John 3

    ii. The woman at the well – John 4

    iii. The woman caught in adultery – John 8

    iv. The one repentant thief on a cross

    v. The one woman with the dead son

3. Now we know why Jesus was concerned about <u>every ONE</u>.

Lesson 57

"The Parable of the Lost Coin"

Luke 15:8-10

I.   THE BACKGROUND OF THE PARABLE
   - A. To explain Jesus' association with tax collectors and sinners
   - B. To rebuke and refute the criticism of the Pharisees and teachers of Israel

II.   THE MEANING OF A PARABLE
   - A. A simple, easily understood earthly story with a heavenly meaning
   - B. A God-truth spoken in the language of the day
     1. Didn't God become a man?
     2. There is overwhelming evidence of the historical Jesus.

III. THE MESSAGE OF THIS PARABLE
   - A. The Parable
     1. A woman has 10 silver coins and loses one of them.
     2. The woman goes all out to find this coin; she succeeds.
     3. The woman calls friends and neighbors together for a rejoicing party.
     4. In a similar way, all of heaven rejoices when one sinner repents.
   - B. The spiritual lessons of this parable
     1. One woman, possibly a widow, is of utmost importance to God.
     2. The coin must be found; it represents one-tenth of

her treasury, her livelihood.

3. What would this loss represent to her? The coin was essential to her life.

4. In this story, the coin represents a person
   a. Created in God's image
   b. Created to reflect God
   c. Created to glorify God

5. The "lost" coin represents humanity's plight – we are spiritually separated from God.

6. We are "lost" because of our sin; and sin was our choice.

7. Our sin is a declaration of our rebellion against God.
   a. We chose our way over God's way.
   b. We chose death over life. (Romans 6:23; John 10:10)

8. God acted to prevent this separation from Him.
   a. He came to this world.
   b. He demonstrated and proclaimed who He is.
   c. He died on the cross for our sin.
   d. He took our sin upon Himself.
   e. He arose from the dead, and is alive forevermore.
   f. He commissioned us believers to proclaim this good news to all people.
   g. He saves all who truly believe in Him.
   h. He provides heaven as our eternal home.

Lesson 58

"The Unconditional Love of God the Father"

Luke 15:11-32

I. THE SON LOST IN THE WORLD (vv. 11-24)
   A. The reason for this parable (Luke 15:1-2)
      1. The fact that Jesus welcomed tax collectors and "sinners"
      2. The criticism of the Pharisees and the teachers of the law
   B. The younger son
      1. The estate was worth more to him than his relationship to his father.
      2. He thought that the grass was greener on the other side.
      3. The son rebelled against his father. Why?
      4. A distant country: near or far, the lost person is separated from the father. (see Isaiah 59:2)
      5. The son had a "wildness" in his heart. (see Mark 7:20-23)
      6. He squandered (lavish, waste, dissipate) his money; easy come, easy go.
      7. When we run away from God, a famine is coming.
      8. He hit the bottom of the barrel.
         a. A Jew feeding pigs?
         b. Lavish living makes one very hungry.
      9. He repented (turned from his rebellion). (vv. 17-20)

II. THE SON LOST AT HOME (vv. 25-30)

A. The older son represents the Jews who were satisfied with their religion without Jesus.
1. He was satisfied with his "old wine" faith.
2. He had it made; no risks.
3. He had religion.
   a. Assumed that the "Father of long ago" had correct interpretations
   b. Understood the letter of the law, but not the spirit of the law
B. The older son resents the Father's attitude and action.
1. He refused to try to understand.
2. He really felt like a slave in his Father's house.
3. He obeyed with resentment.
4. He wouldn't have enjoyed a party if his Father gave it.
5. He referred to this brother as "your son".
6. He prejudged his brother: "prostitutes".

III. THE FATHER'S LOVE FOR BOTH SONS (various verses; vv. 31-32)
A. The Father (God) is always more than ready for a child to make a U-turn homeward.
1. Saw him at a long distance
2. Filled with compassion
   a. Ran
   b. Hugged
   c. Kissed him
B. The Father heard his penitent statement; didn't chastise his son.
C. The Father started the party, a VIP.
D. The Father saw the son:
1. As dead; now alive

    2. As lost; now found

E. The Father was more joyful than the son. Why?

F. The Father doesn't overlook anyone.

G. The older brother just didn't get it.

    1. He didn't know who he was.

    2. He didn't know whose he was.

Lesson 59

"The Shrewd Manager"

Luke 16:1-15

I. THE DISHONEST MANAGER (vv. 1-7)
    A. The manager was the C.F.O. of the company (Chief Financial Officer).
        1. Was guilty of embezzlement (stealing, taking by fraud)
        2. The company owner learned of this deed, and called him in to account for it.
        3. The owner fired him.
        4. Numbers 32:23
    B. The manager quickly devised a shrewd plan.
        1. He recognized his weaknesses. (2 Corinthians 12:7-10)
        2. He devised a plan to win friends and influence people.

II. THE DECEITFUL PHARISEES (vv. 14-15)
    A. Definition: deceivers; snakes in the grass, hypocrites; swindlers; imposters
    B. They loved money. (1 Timothy 6:6-10)
    C. They sneered at, and hated Jesus because his words and life convicted them.
    D. They had religion, but not God.
    E. Religious people make our job (as witnesses for Christ) hard.

III. THE DIVINE MASTER: JESUS
    A. Definition (of Divine): the creator; the Supreme being;

the first cause (I am); the infinite one; the eternal one;
the all-powerful; the all-wise; the all-knowing;
sovereignty; the messiah; the Saviour; the judge;
Immanuel; the way; the door; the truth; the Life; and
other adjectives

B. The human master (owner of the company)
   commended the shrewd manager.

C. Jesus did not approve the manager's actions.

D. Jesus said they (worldly people) were wiser than the
   children of light.

E. The godly givers receive eternal gifts.

F. Our management of money and possessions determines
   our true wealth. (See Luke 6:38)

G. We simply cannot love God and Mammon (money or
   material possessions).

Lesson 60

"The Law and the Prophets on Adultery"

Luke 16:16-18

I.   THE LAW AND THE PROPHETS (vv. 16-17)
- A. Refers to the entire Old Testament
- B. John the Baptist marked the end of the Old Testament era. Jesus marked the beginning of the new Testament era.
- C. "Everyone is forcing his way into it" (some versions) can be translated "everyone is strongly urged"; probably refers to the urgency of John the Baptist and Jesus to repent, believe, and receive Jesus as Saviour and Lord, thereby entering the Kingdom of God.

II.   ADULTERY AND DIVORCE (v. 18)
- A. Remarriage after divorce is adultery if the former marriage was dissolved for illegitimate reasons.
- B. See Matthew 5:31-32 and 19:9. These indicate that remarriage is legitimate in cases where the former marriage was dissolved due to sexual immorality.
- C. Married couples should consider the spirit of the law and not just the letter of the law.

III.   GENERAL TEACHINGS ON ADULTERY
- A. Exodus 20:14 – the 7th Commandment
- B. Matthew 5:27 – begins with lust
- C. The deadly nature of adultery (Proverbs 6:20-35; 7:1-27)
- D. There is no end to the evil of adultery. (Mark 6:14-29)
- E. Where does adultery originate? (Mark 7:14-23)

F. Results of adultery:
1. Break up of families; divorce
2. The extreme hurt of the single parent; usually the mother
3. Dead-beat dads
4. The fatherless home
5. Latch-key youth
6. Shame and guilt
7. Financial dependence on entitlements
G. How can we fight this evil?
1. Teach and drill in the hearts of our children:
   a. The meaning of marriage
   b. Marriage is for one man and one woman till death parts them. (Matthew 19:3-9)
   c. Teach and drill in the church's doctrine that a Christian should not be unequally yoked. (2 Corinthians 6:14-7:1)
   d. Teach the sin of trial marriage.
   e. Teach that the marriage relationship is a triangular affair: God at the apex – Lord of the marriage; man and woman are at the left and right angles.
2. Lead our children and youth to Christ as Saviour and Lord:
   a. They must be saved – born again.
   b. They must understand the meaning of the body (holy) and the peace and joy that comes with following God's teachings. (I Corinthians 6:12-20)
   c. Marriage must be a holy attachment of a man and woman; and dissolved only by death.

d. Warn them of the dangers of peer pressure.

e. Parents must be godly models of marriage.

f. Children must learn that they cannot have adult devices and freedom.

H. Teach our children the meaning of salvation: (I Corinthians 15:1-4)

1. Our sin debt to God is paid in full.

2. We become transformed people.

3. The Lord lives within us.

4. Our sin can be forgiven.

5. Salvation is by grace through faith, and not of works. (Ephesians 2:8-10)

6. A model for husband/wife relationship is found in Ephesians 5:22-33.

IV. YOUR THOUGHTS, SUGGESTIONS, ADDITIONS, QUESTIONS:

A. _____

B. _____

C. _____

D. _____

Lesson 61

"Two Choices for Life: In This World and The Next World"

Luke 16:19-31

I. PEOPLE: EVERYONE, ANYONE
   A. The rich man
      1. Is not named
      2. Is rich, lived in luxury, had everything he needed?
      3. Was selfish; ignored the needy
      4. Could not see beyond himself
   B. Lazarus: the beggar
      1. Could have been a beggar by his own choices
      2. Likely, was a beggar because he was too ill to care
         for himself
         a. No food; full of sores; longing to eat even the
            crumbs from the table
         b. Was a true believer (v. 23)
      3. Likely, no one cared for him.
   C. Who are you?

II. POSSESSIONS: ALL THAT BELONGS TO YOU
   A. Do people really need luxury?
   B. Why do the "well-off people" often hoard their things?
   C. Why do we often overlook the real needy people?
   D. Where and what are our treasures? (Matthew 6:19-24)
   E. I Chronicles 29:14
   F. Luke 6:38
   G. Acts 20:35
   H. 2 Corinthians 9:7
   I. Do you have too many possessions?

J. Matthew 19:23-24

III. PLACE: IN THIS WORLD; IN THE NEXT WORLD

    A. Am I: "well off"; comfortable; have more than enough; rich; will never need to worry?

    B. Am I: using things God's way; really in need; obedient to God regarding possessions?

    C. Why am I not a tither? 10% for God; 90% for me.

    D. James 1:27; 2:14-17

    E. Is there really another life; a Heaven; a Hell; nothing?

       1. Jesus says there is a heaven and a hell. Both are eternal.

       2. This life is so brief and uncertain. We must decide now.

       3. Earth positions are often reversed in eternity.

       4. Hell: unending woes; suffering; misery; separation – without God.

       5. Hell: immediate concern for lost/unsaved loved ones; and others.

       6. You have two choices: God's Kingdom, or Satan's kingdom.

       7. Heed John 3:16-21, 36; John 5:24.

Lesson 62

"The Christian Life Regarding Sin, Faith, And Duty"

Luke 17:1-10

I. THE CHRISTIAN LIVES IN A WORLD OF SIN. (vv. 1-2)
    A. Sin's origin and nature
       1. Romans 5:12
       2. Psalms 51:5
       3. Romans 3:9-18; 23
       4. Galatians 5:19-21
       5. Romans 6:23
       6. Galatians 5:24
       7. 2 Corinthians 5:21
    B. Sin's development and deceit

II. THE CHRISTIAN LIVES BY FAITH FROM ANOTHER WORLD. (vv. 3-6)
    A. Faith is God's gift to all.
       1. Romans 10:8-10
       2. Romans 10:17
    B. Faith and forgiveness

III. THE CHRISTIAN LIVES BY FAITH WHICH IS EXPECTED. (vv. 7-10)
    A. The example of the servant and the master
    B. Doing what God says is only doing our duty.
    C. The Christian must never forget that he is an unworthy servant.

Lesson 63

"The Healed but Not Whole"

Luke 17:11-19

I.   THE HOPELESS

    A. Ten men with leprosy

    B. Characteristics of leprosy:

        1. Disfigurement of the body's extremities

        2. A wasting away of the body

        3. A disease often unknown to the victim

        4. A contagious disease

    B. Their hopeless attitude:

        1. No doctor nor medicine could heal it.

        2. Others excluded them.

        3. The outcome was obvious.

        4. Life was isolated and lonely.

II.   THE HEALER

    A. The "Great Physician" was passing through.

        1. The Jews and Samaritans hated and avoided each other.

        2. Jesus neither hated nor avoided anyone.

           a. He is God; created us all.

           b. To Him, no one was untouchable.

        3. He was at the right place at the right time.

        4. The meeting was not coincidental.

    B. The lepers had heard of Him.

        1. That He was the Saviour

        2. And the Master (teacher)

    C. Jesus always responds when called upon.

1. He hears our cry for help.
2. Isaiah 55:6; 65:1; Luke 19:10; Romans 10:20

III.   THE HEALED

A. The Lord spoke; they were healed.
B. Healing was instantaneous.
C. The "Great Physician" created with a word; healed with a word.
D. Let's hand it to them; all ten obeyed His orders.
E. Alas the nine were concerned only about their bodies.
F. Only one, a Samaritan, came back to the healer.
G. Did the nine not even consider who healed them?
H. Was only one made WHOLE: body, soul, and spirit?
I. Where did the nine go? What did they think and feel about Jesus? Did the physical miracle do anything spiritually to them? Did they ever become whole?
J. Questions for me. Eternal ones.
1. Is body health of supreme importance?
2. Have I thought about: when this/that happens to me, what do I do?
3. Am I really secure when I am healthy, wealthy, and wise?
4. Am I concerned about the "beyond the physical" existence?
5. What do you believe about the "after life"?

Lesson 64

"The Coming of the Kingdom of God"

Luke 17:20-37

I. WHAT IS THE KINGDOM OF GOD?
    A. The reign or rule of God in your life (v. 21)
    B. God will be a Father to the true believers. (2 Corinthians 6:18)
    C. Eternal life with the Father in a real, physical place

II. WHEN IS THE KINGDOM OF GOD PRESENT?
    A. When a person receives Christ in his heart
    B. One who honors the Father and keeps His word
    C. One who believes the truth that Christ taught, thus honoring the Father (John 8:12-59)
    D. At a future point in time the King shall be seen by all. (Luke 17:22-29)

III. WHO WILL BE IN THE KINGDOM OF GOD?
    A. The Father of all who believe (Romans 4:11)
    B. John 1:12; 20:29
    C. John 3:36; 5:24

IV. WHAT WILL HAPPEN WHEN THE KING APPEARS?
    A. Life will be normal, as in the days of Noah. (vv. 26-27)
    B. Life will go on as in Lot's day as usual, just before the awful judgment comes on the unbelievers. (vv. 28-29)
    C. When the Son of Man is revealed, people will show where their treasures are. "Remember Lot's wife."
    D. Lot's wife looked back, with longing, on her former life, and judgment came swiftly. (vv. 30-32)

E. The unbeliever will lose his real life because he tried to keep what belonged to the old, sinful self. The believer will keep his new life, because he gave up what was worthless. (v. 33)

F. Two people, who appear to be alike, will be separated for all eternity. God knows the heart. (vv. 34-35)

Lesson 65

"The Parable of the Persistent Widow"

Luke 18:1-8

I.   THE PERSISTENCY OF PRAYER
   A. Matthew 7:8-9
   B. Matthew 26:36-46
   C. The early Christians prayed, then acted.
   D. Paul prayed three times about his thorn in the flesh.

II.   THE SPECIFICITY OF PRAYER
   A. The widow came to the judge over and over again, about the same thing.
   B. Paul prayed about the "thorn in the flesh".
   C. Jesus prayed about the "cup of suffering".

III.   THE POWER OF PRAYER
   A. 2 Chronicles 7:14
   B. 2 Chronicles 30:27
   C. Fasting and prayer often work together. (Ezra 8:23)
   D. Obedience to God will keep your prayers from being hindered.
   E. The prayer of faith in the church (James 5:13-20)

Lesson 66

"The Parable of the Pharisee and the Tax Collector"

Luke 18:9-14

I.   THE SELF-RIGHTEOUS PHARISEE
   A. Confident of his own righteousness
   B. Looked down, with disdain, on everybody else
   C. He went to the Temple to pray.
   D. He prayed about himself.
    1. Bragged that he was not like other men
      a. A robber
      b. An evil-doer
      c. An adulterer
      d. Nor even like the tax collector
    2. Bragged about the positive things he did
      a. Fasted twice a week
      b. Gave a tenth of all he got
   E. Isaiah 64:6 – like filthy rags
   F. Romans 3:9-12 – no one is good
   G. Isaiah 53:4-6 – if we are righteous, on our own, why did Jesus suffer and die for our sins?
   H. Ephesians 2:1-10 – All, who are not saved by the blood, are dead in our sins.

II.   THE SELF-EFFACED TAX COLLECTOR
   A. How the tax collector saw himself
    1. Stood at a distance
    2. Not worthy to look up to heaven
    3. Beat his breast
    4. Talked to God

5. Asked for mercy

6. Admitted he was a sinner

B. How John the Baptist saw himself (John 1:26-27)

1. How Isaiah saw himself (Isaiah 6:1-5)

2. How Paul saw himself (1Timothy 1:15)

III.   THE SELF-GIVING GOD

A. How John the Baptist saw Jesus (John 3:36; John 1:29)

B. How Jesus saw Himself (Luke 19:10; John 3:36)

C. How Paul saw the need of the Saviour, for everyone

1. Romans 3:19-31

2. Romans 4:1-10

D. A re-assuring re-statement by Jesus about who He knew He was (John 5:24)

Lesson 67

"Jesus and the Little Children"

Luke 18:15-17

I.   PEOPLE IN GENERAL SAW A NEED TO BRING LITTLE CHILDREN TO JESUS.
   A. For Him to Touch Them
      1. So that they would be healed?
      2. So that His spiritual power might touch them?
      3. To introduce them to the most amazing person of all time?
   B. The Disciples Rebuked Them.
      1. Did they rebuke the children, or the adults who brought them?
      2. Why would they do this?

II. JESUS RESPONDED POSITIVELY TO CHILDREN.
   A. He called them to Himself.
   B. He encouraged people to let them come and not hinder.
   C. How do we hinder the children from coming to Him?
   D. Our hindrances. We do not:
      1. Realize that we are responsible to God for them
      2. Pray with them, nor in their presence
      3. Take them to church regularly
      4. Try to lead them to Christ
      5. Discipline them
      6. Spend quality time with them, nor do we learn from them their needs
      7. Hug and love on them enough
      8. Pay attention to their friends

E. Our hindrances. We do:
1. Set ungodly examples before them
2. Preach, but don't practice our preaching
3. Allow them to make choices, when they are not capable of doing so
4. Allow them too much freedom
5. Do something and refuse that same privilege to them

F. What else?
1. We do not:
    a. _____
    b. _____
    c. _____
    d. _____
2. We do:
    a. _____
    b. _____
    c. _____
    d. _____

III. JESUS SAID, "THE KINGDOM OF GOD BELONGS TO SUCH AS THESE."
A. Anyone who goes to heaven must respond as the children do.
1. In real, believing faith
2. In total dependence
3. Just as they are
4. With real emotions

B. The traits of a child. Characteristics:
1. Trust
2. Love
3. Innocence

4. Lack of power
5. Lack of credentials
6. Lack of pretension
7. Forgiving
8. Unknown

C. The <u>ONLY</u> ones who can enter the kingdom are the "child-like faith" ones.
  1. Childlikeness is giving your total self to God.
  2. A true child of God must give up their:
    a. Pretensions
    b. Selfishness
    c. Greed
    d. Claims to fame
    e. The need to control
    f. Grasp for power
    g. Ideas that God's Laws don't matter
    h. Vanity
    i. Self-assurance

D. Whom did Jesus seek as disciples?
  1. The poor
  2. Women
  3. Samaritans
  4. Children
  5. Disabled ones
  6. Tax collectors
  7. Sinners
  8. Humble people
  9. The hearers of God's word

Lesson 68

"Jesus and the Rich Young Ruler"

Luke 18:18-30

I. THE RICH YOUNG RULER
   A. He had much in his favor.
      1. Young
      2. A ruler
      3. Rich
      4. Had lived a moral life: keeping five of the Ten Commandments – according to his understanding (Commandments #5, 6, 7, 8, 9)
   B. He knew something was missing in his life.
      1. Knew whom to find the answer
      2. Revered and respected Jesus

II. JESUS CHRIST
   A. Concerned about everyone: rich; poor; educated; uneducated; rulers and slaves; young and old
   B. Gave an audience to anyone desiring it
      1. Never showed partiality
      2. Knows our hearts, and still loves us
   C. The Master Teacher
      1. Conversations were not trivial
      2. He communicated by questions.
      3. He led people by interchanging conversations – not one-way.
      4. He always led people to truth. (v. 29)
      5. He knows what we are hiding from Him, but leads and loves anyway.

III. THE QUESTION OF THE RICH YOUNG RULER
   A. "What must I do to inherit eternal life?"
      1. Knew he needed eternal life
      2. Saw salvation as something to be earned
         a. Romans 3:9-20; 4:1-10
         b. Ephesians 2:8-10
   B. The Ruler must understand the LAW vs. GRACE
      THROUGH FAITH.

IV. THE ANSWER OF JESUS
   A. With a question, "Why do you call me good?"
      1. No one is good, but God.
      2. Jesus wanted the ruler to see that He is God – not just a man.
   B. He reminded the ruler of only five of the Ten Commandments.
   C. Note the commandments that Jesus left out: #1, #2, #3, #4, #10.
   D. The ruler saw life as a relationship between people and people – only.
   E. (VIP) The ruler lacked one thing: Who or What was God in his life?
   F. Jesus led the ruler to see what was God in his life: riches – money – possessions. (vv. 22-25)
   G. Jesus told the ruler what he should do.
      1. Sell all he had and give all to the poor
      2. And, to follow Jesus
   H. The ruler walked away, very sad. (Mark 10:17-31)
   I. The answer of Jesus poses lots of questions for us.
      1. Do we have to give away everything?
      2. Can the rich go to Heaven?
      3. Let's find the answers.

4. Real life is worth all and more of us than this world can offer.

Lesson 69

"Jesus Predicts His Death"

Luke 18:31-34

I. JESUS PREDICTS HIS DEATH.
    A. He shares this with the twelve disciples.
    B. It will be fulfilled in Jerusalem.
    C. Everything written by the prophets will be fulfilled.
       1. Calls Himself the Son of Man
       2. Will be handed over to the Gentiles, who will mock Him, insult Him, spit on Him, flog Him, and kill Him
       3. He will rise from the dead on the third day.

II. THE DISCIPLES DID NOT UNDERSTAND HIS MESSAGE.

III. THE PROPHECIES FULFILLED IN JESUS
    A. Psalm 2:1-2, 4-6, 8-12
    B. Isaiah 50:6-7; Isaiah 52:13-53:12
    C. Daniel 7:13-14
    D. Zephaniah 3:11-12
    E. Luke 9:21-22, 44-45; Luke 12:49-50; Luke 13:32-35; Luke 17:25
    F. Micah 5:2 – Would be born in Bethlehem

Lesson 70

"Jesus Meets a Blind Beggar"

Luke 18:35-43

I.   JESUS APPROACHES JERICHO.

II.   A BLIND BEGGAR LEARNS THAT JESUS IS
      PASSING BY.
      A. He learns that Jesus is in the crowd.
      B. He calls on Jesus to have mercy on him.
      C. He is rebuked by leaders.
      D. He is determined to meet Jesus, and calls for mercy
         again.

III. JESUS RESPONDS TO THE NEED.
      A. He takes charge and orders others to bring the man to
         Him.
      B. He inquires of the beggar about his need.
      C. He recognizes the beggar's faith, and heals him of
         blindness.
      D. His action elicited praise and new followers.

IV.   JESUS' MIRACLES SYMBOLIZE GREATER
      TRUTHS.
      A. The blind beggar receiving sight symbolizes the
         spiritual light that God gives to us. (John 1:4-5)
      B. The feeding of the 5000 symbolizes that Jesus is the
         bread of life. (John 6:27; 45-47)
      C. The boy in sign two above shows that no matter how
         little we have to offer God is what we should do.
      D. The story of the Centurion in Matthew 8:5-13, and
         Jesus healing his servant shows that space is no

problem with Him.

E. The story of Jesus raising Lazarus from the dead shows His power over death, and signifies His own resurrection. (John 11)

F. The real lessons are two-fold.

1. The sight-restored indicates an eternal healing of the body.

2. See John 9:35-41. "the blind will see and those who see will become blind." (v. 39)

Lesson 71

"Jesus and Zacchaeus"

Luke 19:1-10

I.   ZACCHAEUS, THE CROOKED TAX COLLECTOR
   A. Who he was:
      1. From the town of Jericho; wealthy
      2. A crooked Jew working for the Roman government
         a. Made his income by hook or crook
         b. Set the amount; charged more than the people owed
         c. Stuffed the overage in his pockets
   B. Whom he desired to be
      1. In everyone, there is a revelation of God. (Romans 1:18-20)
      2. Some people do not think it worthwhile to retain the knowledge of God. (Romans 1:28)
      3. A true believer
   C. Whom he came to be
      1. Went to the source of salvation
      2. Welcomed Jesus gladly
      3. Listened to the Lord
         a. He believed. (a son of Abraham)
         b. He repented. (admitted his dishonesty)

II.   THE PEOPLE: THE CRITICAL JUDGES
   A. The crowd observed Jesus carefully.
   B. The crowd noted where He went.
   C. The people judged Jesus and Zacchaeus.
      a. That Jesus should not visit a known sinner

      b. That Zacchaeus was like all other tax collectors

D. Why do we judge?

    1. Jesus warns against this. (Matthew 7:1-5)

    2. James warns against this. (James 2:1-4)

    3. Then why?

III. <u>JESUS, THE COMPASSIONATE SAVIOUR</u>

A. Jesus finds people who are seeking Him. (v. 3)

B. Jesus finds people who are not looking for Him. (John 4 – the woman at the well)

C. Jesus' mission is to seek and save the lost. (v. 10)

D. Jesus was not partial in whom He chose.

    1. Poor and rich

    2. Ignorant and educated

    3. Healthy and sick

    4. Children, youth, and adults

E. Jesus set up appointments, or witnessed on the spot.

Lesson 72

"The Parable of the Ten Minas"

Luke 19:11-27

I. INTRODUCTION
    A. A mina equaled approximately a pound of money.
    B. This parable could be titled "The Parable of the Ten Pounds".
    C. Jesus used weights and measures to describe gifts, values, and worth, money.
       1. Mina; pound; kesitah; shekel; bekah; talent
       2. A talent weighed about 3000 shekels.
    D. The parable: a response to the people thinking the kingdom of God was to come at once
       1. Jesus – going to Jerusalem
       2. Jesus: the man of noble birth
       3. The ten servants: representative of all people
       4. The mina: representative of God's gifts for responsibility

II. JESUS: THE TRUE KING OF THIS WORLD
    A. Galatians 4:4-7
    B. Matthew 2:1-2
    C. The claims of Jesus
       1. That God was His Father: John 8:12-30
       2. That He was the Son of God: John 8
       3. That He was the Son of Man: John 9:35-39
    D. He created all things and everything belongs to Him.
    E. His life and works demonstrated that He is the King of Kings – the One and only God.

F. His Kingdom is not of this world. (John 18:36)

G. Regarding Jesus, there is a choice.
  1. Joshua 24:14-15
  2. John 3:36

H. Regarding Jesus, there is a consequence.
  1. John 3:36; 5:24
  2. I John 5:13

III. SATAN: THE WOULD-BE KING OF THIS WORLD

A. Who he is:
  1. Revelation 12:7-17
  2. 2 Corinthians 4:3-4

B. Who his servants are:
  1. The hypocrites
  2. Those who choose themselves over Christ
    a. The Rich Young Ruler
    b. Herod
    c. Pilate
  3. Those who live a habitual life of transgressing the Lord's commandments (II Peter 2:4-19)
  4. The atheists
  5. Those who hate Jesus
  6. Those who reject Christ's Lordship

C. What options do his servants have?
  1. A choice to reject the Lord
  2. A choice to receive the Lord
  3. A choice to live forever
  4. A choice to die forever
  5. The saddest sight: the choice to love this world (I John 2:15-17)

Lesson 73

"The Entry of Jesus Into Jerusalem"

Luke 19:28-48

I.   HIS PREPARATION (vv. 28-34)
   A. His destiny: Jerusalem: not accidental nor coincidental
      (Luke 13:33)
   B. His disciples' role

II. HIS PURPOSE (Luke 19:35; 43-44)
   A. To ride on a colt to fulfill prophecy (Zechariah 9:9)
   B. To reveal Himself as their true king
   C. To announce this crucial event
   D. To fulfill His mission
   E. To predict the future of the Jews

III. HIS PRIORITIES (vv. 39-40)
   A. To announce that nothing could stop His mission
   B. To show the true purpose of the temple
   C. To purify the temple

IV. HIS PRAISE (vv. 37-38; 48)
   A. The crowd of disciples unashamedly for the miracles
      He had performed
   B. The crowd by hanging on His every word

V.   HIS PAIN
   A. He wept when He saw the city.
   B. He wept because they chose not to understand what
      really mattered.
   C. He wept because He knew their hearts were hardened.

Lesson 74

"Jesus: Lord of All"

Luke 20:1-19

I.   THE TEACHER HAS ALL AUTHORITY. (vv. 1-8)

    A. The Jewish leaders asked about the authority of Jesus to do what He was doing.

        1. Always trying to catch Him in error

        2. Wanted to know where He got his authority

        3. Needed an acceptable reason

    B. The Lord (Teacher) answered with a question.

        1. About the authority of the baptism of John

        2. Either answer put them in jeopardy.

        3. The Jews couldn't answer; He would not answer.

    C. The Lord's works proved His authority.

        1. His teaching

        2. His attributes: omniscience; omnipotence; omnipresence; immortality; immutability; etc.

II.   THE TITLE-HOLDER OWNS EVERYTHING.

    A. Jesus represents the Title-Holder of the vineyard.

    B. The Title-Holder is rich – oh, how rich!

        1. He is the creator. (Colossians 1:15-16)

        2. He is the sustainer of all things. (Colossians 1:17)

        3. He visited the earth, and became a man. (Galatians 4:4; John 1:10-14)

        4. His rich life is given to us. (John 10:10)

    C. The Title-Holder goes away.

        1. He rents the farm to tenants.

            a. Gives them authority

b. Expects a return from the production

D. The Title-Holder goes away for a long time. (John 14:1-3; Acts 1:6-11)

1. He will return to the earth – the second coming.

2. He is patient and long-suffering with the tenants. (2 Peter 3:8-9)

III. THE TENANTS ARE RESPONSIBLE TO THE TITLE-HOLDER.

A. The tenants are the Jews, the chosen people.

1. They reject the Owner (the Lord).

2. They devise a plan to get rid of Him.

3. The leaders are often followed blindly.

4. The people must always count the cost of following the One in charge.

B. The tenants had no interest in the Owner.

1. Did not respect His ownership

2. Persecuted the servants of the owner; and the Son

C. The tenants' character

1. Selfish; greedy; evil; "burger-king" men (have it your way)

2. Foolish: did they really think they would get away with this?

Lesson 75

"Trying to Overcome Good with Evil"

Luke 20:20-26

I.   <u>DECEIT OF EVIL MEN</u>

    A. Deceit goes after the top of Good: Jesus.

        1. If you topple the King, you destroy the Kingdom.

        2. Ironic: they knew who the king was.

    B. Deceit stops for nothing in trying to achieve their mission.

        1. They sent their spies to watch the <u>ONE</u> who had nothing to hide.

        2. They produced false witnesses.

        3. They mocked and lied about the <u>ONE</u> who is the most desirable of the ages.

    C. Deceit can be stopped only by truth.

II.   <u>DECLARATION OF GOD'S TRUTH BY JESUS</u>

    A. The evil leaders knew that Jesus always spoke and acted in truth and honesty.

        1. Verses 21-22

        2. John 8:31-32

    B. The Lord Jesus sees the duplicity of the heart.

        1. John 2:23-25

        2. What's in the heart is the origin of evil. (Mark 7:5-8)

    C. The Lord Jesus reversed their trap by undeniable example. (vv. 23-25)

III.   <u>DESTINY OF GOD-DENIERS</u>

    A. They will be silenced by the Lord's truth. (v. 26)

B. Matthew 23
1. They keep others from heaven and don't go there themselves. (v. 13)
2. They are sons of hell, and lead others to be worse than they are. (v. 15)
3. They acted clean, but in their hearts they were full of greed. (v. 25)
4. How would they escape hell? (v. 33)
5. Peter speaks clearly of their destiny. (2 Peter 2:1-3)
C. Who are God-deniers today?
1. False members in churches
2. Atheists deny God's existence.
3. Agnostics say that we cannot know God exists.
4. "Cultural Christian" church members who are never involved in God's kingdom, but want the benefits of the name.
5. Unsaved church leaders with ulterior motives
D. Is there any hope for God-deniers? Yes
1. In Christ through repentance and faith
2. By being born again
3. By knowing and following the truth revealed in God's word (Matthew 7:21-23)
4. By becoming a new person in Christ (2 Corinthians 5:17)

Lesson 76

"Group Opposition to Jesus"

Luke 20:27-40

I.   THE SADDUCEES ACCUSE JESUS. (vv. 27-33)
   A. Nothing new about this
      1. They and other religious groups always attacked the truth.
      2. Religion is man's attempt to find God. Christianity reveals God coming to man.
   B. The main tenets of their religion
      1. They came from the leading families of the nation: priests, merchants, aristocrats, and wealthy people.
      2. They believed that the Torah (first five books of the Old Testament) were binding.
      3. They did not believe in the resurrection of the dead; the immortality of the soul; in rewards or punishments handed out to the dead; nor heaven or hell; nor angels or spirits.
      4. They did not want any changes which might upset their authority; threaten their privileges.
      5. They opposed Jesus as they saw Him as dangerous in their eyes.
   C. Their story of "Levirate Marriage"
      1. A form of marriage in the Law of Moses in which a man was required to marry the widow of a brother who died with no male heir (Deuteronomy 25:5-10)
      2. They were "blind guides who strained out a gnat

but swallowed a camel". (Matthew 23:24)

II.   THE LORD ANSWERS THE SADDUCEES. (vv. 34-38)

    A. "Levirate Marriage" applies to this age, only.

    B. God's children, the children of the resurrection

        1. Will neither marry nor be given in marriage

        2. Can no longer die

        3. Are like the angels, but not angels

    B. God is the God of Abraham, Isaac, and Jacob – not "was".

    C. God is not the God of the dead, but of the living.

        1. Matthew 17:1-8

        2. John 11:25-26

III.   THE SADDUCESS ACCEPT THE LORD'S ANSWER (vv. 39-40)

    A. There comes a time when we must cease arguing with God – when we have nothing to say.

    B. The Sadducees were wise to hush, lest they be further embarrassed among their peers.

Lesson 77

"Hypocritical Teachers of the Law"

Luke 20:41-47

I.   JESUS ILLUSTRATED THEIR FALSE INTERPRETATION.
   A. The original quote: Psalm 110:1
   B. Matthew's version of this story: Matthew 22:41-46
   C. The Ongoing Battle Between the Flesh and the Spirit:
      1. The Jewish leaders were teachers of the fleshly way: Galatians 5:17; Ephesians 2:3; Romans 8:8; Galatians 5:19-23.
      2. Jesus taught by the Spirit of God.
         a. The Holy Spirit is the Spirit of Jesus. (2 Corinthians 3:17)
         b. A person relates to Jesus only by means of the Holy Spirit. (Romans 8:9; Galatians 4:6)

II. JESUS INDICTS THEM REGARDING HYPOCRISY.
   A. Verses 45-47 are expanded and amplified in Matthew 23.
   B. Teachers of the Law and Pharisees are charged with many forms of hypocrisy in Matthew 23.
      1. They burden the common people with hundreds of man-made religious laws, but do not practice them. (v. 4)
      2. Their religion is practiced as a show for man to see. (vv. 5-7)
         a. They enrich and embellish their religious clothing.

b. They seek places of honor for show.

   c. They love titles and greetings of man.

3. They will not enter the kingdom and they bar the door to the kingdom for others. (vv. 13-14)

4. They travel over land and sea to win a convert, and make him a worse son of hell than they are. (v. 15)

5. They are blind guides and blind fools who lead others to twist the law to their advantage. (vv. 16-22)

6. They tithe of even minor things, and neglect more important matters of the Law. (vv. 23-24)

   a. They should tithe.

   b. They should not neglect matters of the mind and heart.

7. The outside of their lives sparkle, but the inside (the heart) is corrupt. (vv. 25-28)

8. They exalt their evil forbears, but practice their actions and teachings. (vv. 29-32)

9. The Accusation of Jesus and the Terror That Follows Hypocrisy (vv. 33-36)

Lesson 78

"God's Teaching About Money, Wealth, and Riches"

Luke 21:1-4

I. JESUS SEES THE HEART (THE MOTIVE) OF MONEY, WEALTH, AND RICHES.
    A. He saw how the rich contributed.
    B. He saw how the poor Godly woman gave.

II. THE SPIRITUAL MEANING OF MONEY AND RICHES
    A. Wealth Comes from God. (Proverbs 3:9-10)
        1. Who owns everything?
        2. Who gives us what we need?
    B. The only Jewish coin mentioned in the New Testament is the widow's mite (or lepton), a copper coin worth only a fraction of a penny by today's standards. (Luke 21:1-4)
        1. Prior to coins, there was a barter system.
        2. Other Greek and Roman coins are mentioned in the New Testament: a denarius; a mina; a talent.
    C. General teachings on wealth from Proverbs: Proverbs 10:15, 13:11, 19:4
    D. Measurements of the use of wealth (Amos 2:6-7)
    E. The possession of wealth is not always the sign of God's favor. (Jeremiah 12:1)
    F. Jesus speaks: the most VIP passage in the Bible regarding wealth. (Matthew 6:19-21, 24)

III. THE SPRITUAL MEANING OF BEING RICH AND THE USE OF RICHES

A. Money and Riches must be used for the glory of God. (1 Chronicles 21:22-26)
B. We must love God supremely and love others as ourselves, and use money and riches. (1 Chronicles 29:10-14)
   1. Not use others
   2. Not hoard money
C. Dishonest practices of weighing were banned because a false balance is abhorrent (hated and despised) by the Lord. (Proverbs 11:1)
D. What people will do for money (Matthew 26:14-16)
E. The tragedy of choosing Satan's way over God's way: the Rich young Ruler (Mark 10:17-27)
F. The blindness regarding God's truth and reality: the Rich man and Lazarus (Luke 16:19-31)
G. The rich almost always love their money. (1 Timothy 6:3-10)
H. The only true and lasting wealth is the spiritual riches of God's Kingdom. (Matthew 13:44-46)

Lesson 79

"The Study of End Times on Earth; and Our Eternal Preparation for the Future"

Luke 21:5-38

I. THE DISCIPLES' QUESTION TO JESUS ABOUT THE TEMPLE (vv. 5-6)
   A. Jesus deals first with the Temple in Jerusalem.
   B. This event would happen in their life-time: A.D 70; the Roman Army's destruction of the Temple.

II. JESUS' TEACHING ABOUT END-TIMES IS RECORDED IN MATTHEW 24; MARK 13; AND OUR TEXT IN LUKE 21:7-8.
   A. Verse 8: The Lord warned about false TEACHERS.
   B. Jesus instructed us: "Don't follow them."
   C. Verses 9-10: Wars and rumors of wars will take place; nations will war against one another. Not a certain sign of the end.
   D. Verse 11: Disturbances in nature; and signs in the sky may happen again and again.
   E. Verses 12-19
      1. Persecution will occur on account of the name of Jesus.
      2. Persecution will result in our being witnesses to the persecutors.
      3. Betrayal by family members
      4. Some will die.
      5. Persecution for Jesus will not be eternal. (v. 18)

F. Verses 20-24
1. Instructions by Jesus regarding what to do when devastation comes to Jerusalem
2. This will happen until the times of the Gentiles will be fulfilled.

G. Verses 25-26
1. Will be signs in the sun, moon, and stars
2. The seas will roar and toss and people will experience terror regarding what they see.

H. Verses 27-32
1. The people of earth will see Jesus coming back in Glory from Heaven to earth.
2. Jesus came the first time as a lamb of God; He will return in Kingly power.
3. The believers will look up to the skies, knowing their pilgrim journey is over, and their perfectly redeemed life is about to begin.
4. Verse 32: "This generation" surely must refer to the generation alive when the above events take place.

III. JESUS' ASSURANCES AND WARNINGS REGARDING BEING READY FOR HIS RETURN
A. Verse 33: This physical earth will pass away, but His words will never pass away.
B. Verse 34: Be sure to prepare yourself for the end-time events.
C. Verse 34: Drunken parties and stress will lead to concentration on earth only, and you forget that this world is not eternal.
1. Some people are deceived by Satan.

2. Some people must know that "we must get ready for His coming".

D. Our response:
1. Be sober in your watching for the Lord.
2. Pray always; for strength and protection for the last days; that you will put first things first; that we will trust God for now and eternity; study and trust God's words.

Lesson 80

"The Last Events of Jesus' Earthly Ministry"

Luke 22:1-38

I. THE PASSOVER (THE FEAST OF UNLEAVENED BREAD)
   A. The first of the three great festivals of the Hebrew people
   B. Observed the 14th day of Abib, the first month; the day the Hebrews left Egyptian bondage
   C. The blood on the door posts was a sign to God to "pass over" their houses when He destroyed the first-born of men and animals of Egypt.
   D. Unleavened bread was used to show that the people had no time for the leaven to work as they left in haste.

II. THE PREPARATION FOR THE LORD'S SUPPER
   A. The Lord chose Peter and John to make the preparations.
   B. The Passover meal (the Lord's Supper for us) is eaten where God chooses. (Deuteronomy 16:2)
   C. The lamb was chosen before the 14th of Abib.
   D. This is never to be done haphazardly.

III. THE MEANING OF THE LORD'S SUPPER (OR THE LAST SUPPER) (Luke 22:16)
   A. The Lord's Supper is for disciples of the Lord.
   B. The "Passover Lamb" had to meet very specific requirements. (Exodus 12:1-13)
      1. A male without defects
      2. Certain herbs were used.

       3. A certain cooking method was required.

   C. In the Old Testament sacrificial system, God accepted the blood of animals as the means of atonement for sin.

   D. Jesus is the Lamb of God.

       1. Old Testament references: Isaiah 53:7, 12

       2. New Testament references:

          a. John 1:29, 36

          b. Acts 8:30-35

          c. 1 Peter 1:19

          d. Revelation 5:1-12

   E. References to the "blood of Christ" always mean the sacrificial death of Jesus on the cross.

       1. Leviticus 17:11

       2. Romans 3:21-25A

       3. Ephesians 1:7

       4. I Peter 1:18-19

IV. THE FINAL DECISION OF JUDAS' LIFE

   A. The contract Judas made (vv. 1-6)

   B. The confusion of the disciples

       1. Wondered who the betrayer would be

       2. Had a dispute about which of them was the greatest

       3. Pride was their great downfall. (1 John 2:15-17)

   C. Questions

       1. When is your final decision made?

       2. Is God "a God of second chances"?

       3. Is it ever too late to change your mind?

       4. Your choice about God is, without debate, the most important decision of your life.

V. THE DENIAL OF JESUS

   A. Who is the denier?

   B. Not Peter! Surely, not Peter.

C. Luke 22:31-34
1. Me, the leader
2. Me, the first to confess you
3. Me, "I'm sure I am ready to suffer with you."
4. Me, I walked on water.
5. Peter – over-confident

VI. THE FINAL INSTRUCTIONS (vv. 35-38)

Lesson 81

"The Agony and Surrender of Jesus"

Luke 22:39-53

I.   JESUS SUFFERS AGONY IN PREPARATION FOR
      HIS CRUCIFIXION. (Luke 22:39-46)
      A. Jesus goes to the Mount of Olives (His closet of
         prayer).
      B. Jesus warns the disciples of the real spiritual danger:
         falling into temptation.
      C. Jesus goes deeper into the garden of prayer.
         1. He meets His Father in prayer.
         2. He asks His Father to take the cup of suffering (the
            death on the cross) if it is His will.
            a. He is facing this event as the Son of Man as we
               would.
            b. He is tempted to withdraw from the cross.
            c. The Father provides an angel to strengthen Him.
            d. He prays in anguish about this hour.
         3. Jesus ends His prayer, goes back and finds the
            disciples sleeping and wonders why?
         4. Do you think there was more to His prayer than
            what is recorded?
II.   JESUS SURRENDERS TO THE EVIL AUTHORITIES
      IN PREPARATION FOR THE CRUCIFIXION. (Luke
      22:47-53)
      A. Judas, the betrayer, reveals Himself openly.
         1. Jesus warned of false leaders in the Sermon on the
            Mount. (Matthew 7:15-20)

202

2. Judas did not listen to Jesus with his heart: he loved money; he probably expected a military Messiah.
3. Judas kissed Jesus: a hypocrite?

B. The followers of Jesus responded with worldly wisdom, by human weapons.
   1. Our battles as Christians will never be won with weapons of violence.
   2. The weapons that true believers use
      a. Exodus 14:13-14
      b. 2 Corinthians 10:3-5
      c. Ephesians 6:10-20

C. Jesus confronts the evil leaders with His words.
   1. He healed the servant's ear.
   2. He forgave His enemies.
   3. He explained His methods of warfare.
   4. He defined this event as "their hour of darkness".

Lesson 82

"Three Destructive D's in Peter's Life"

Luke 22:54-62

I. DISTANCE DETERMINES DISCIPLESHIP.

    A. Peter followed Jesus at a distance.

    B. One can be too far behind to hear Jesus' teaching.

    C. We are too far behind Him when:

        1. We have no Bible study.

        2. We skim through the Bible – no study.

        3. We drop out of church.

        4. Church is dull and boring and we choose not to listen to the preacher.

        5. Other things are more important than Jesus: His words; life; and teaching.

    D. Hebrew 10:19-27

        1. It is dangerous to drop out of church.

        2. Two main reasons for dropping out

            a. We are not saved.

            b. The church has failed us.

    E. We are too far behind Jesus, when there are no evidences of discipleship.

        1. When sins are not being conquered

        2. When we know that God is not doing anything in our lives

        3. When we can't hear God

II. DENIAL DENOTES A FALLING AWAY FROM GOD.

    A. What made Peter deny Jesus?

        1. Fear of persecution

      2. Not sure he wanted to deny everything to follow Jesus (Matthew 16:24-26)

      3. Had he boasted too quickly about his willingness to be strong?

      4. Was he not even sure of Jesus?

  B. What are modern reasons for denying Christ?

      1. Fear of persecution

      2. Losing friends

      3. Being rejected

      4. Losing an argument about Jesus

      5. It's my life and I don't want anyone else in control of me.

  C. Which is better?

      1. To have friends and enemies reject you

      2. To have God reject you (Matthew 10:32-33)

      3. You know the answer, don't you?

  D. Peter was rapidly going backwards to his former way of life. (I John 2:15-17)

III.   DISASTER DEVELOPS A LIFE OF CONFUSION, CONTRAST, COALITION, AND COWARDNESS.

  A. When the distance develops between you and God; and denial occurs; then disaster surely follows.

  B. Disaster results in the attack of a spiritual coiling cobra.

      1. The first strike creates a life of confusion.

         a. "I don't believe the Bible."

         b. "I now believe in evolution."

         c. "The government has tried to remove Jesus from our minds."

         d. "There is no God except the one chosen by the individual."

e. "Who's right: my teachers or my parents and preachers?"

f. "I don't know what to believe; I'm confused. I'll just find my inner self."

2. The second strike stings with the deadly poison of contrast.

a. "I'm not like I used to be."

b. "I feel like two different people: as in Dr. Jekyll and Mr. Hyde."

c. "There are two battles going on within me."

d. "I'm doing things that I cannot stop."

3. The third cobra attack leads you to look for a coalition of people like yourself.

a. Leads to finding something you can believe in

b. Join a group or gang where you fit in

c. Do fun things that they do

d. Join the "broadway" gang

e. "I won't be criticized in the gang."

f. Matthew 7:13-14

4. The fourth cobra strike is intended to sink deep.

a. The enemy seeks to destroy from within.

b. The enemy has you now.

c. You say, "I'm too embarrassed to return to Jesus." "I can't measure up."

IV. THERE IS ONE REAL HOPE LEFT.

A. "What can God do for me?"

B. "Have I not really listened to Jesus?"

C. Jesus said:

1. Matthew 11:28-30

2. John 14:6

3. Philippians 4:13

206

4. James 4:7-10

D. "Will God take care of me?" Exodus 14:13-14

E. You can come back! You must make a serious turn. (Isaiah 45:22)

Lesson 83

"The Mock Trial of Jesus Before Pilate and Herod"

Luke 22:63-71

I.   THE PERSONS OF THE PROSECUTION
     A. The Council of the Elders of the Jews
        1. The Sanhedrin Court
        2. Made up of 71 of the Chief Priests and Teachers of the Law
     B. The strategy the Court chose
        1. No trial could be held on the morning of a Feast Day. (i.e. Passover)
        2. Two days were required for capital offenses.
        3. It had to be daylight by law.
           a. In a hurry
           b. No preliminary questions
           c. Their minds made up?
     C. The answer to their questions could lead to blasphemy.
        1. Was He the Christ?
        2. Did they know that Jesus would tell the truth?

II.   THE PERSON OF THE AGES: JESUS
     A. No one had ever seen a person like Him.
        1. Peaceful in a death trial
        2. Non-retaliating in response to persecution
        3. Knew their hearts and motives; as the "Wonderful Counselor", He revealed their hearts. (John 2:24-25)
     B. Jesus knew that the Prosecutors had to hear the truth – before the Crucifixion.

1. He revealed His real home.
2. He revealed who He is.

III. THE PROSECUTORS' PRIME MOTIVE
   A. Looking for false evidence, to put Him to death
   B. No witnesses for the prosecution – strange?
   C. False witnesses found; no real defense
   D. Two witnesses misconstrued a statement Jesus had made. (Matthew 26:59-63)
   E. Jesus refused to answer a false accusation.
      1. They put Him under oath, and He gave them information they did not want.
      2. Their illegal actions got them what they wanted: the death penalty.
   F. The prelude to the cross begins with insults and physical abuse.

Lesson 84

"The Most Noted Trial of Injustice in History"

Luke 23:1-25

I. THE ACCUSATIONS AGAINST JESUS (vv. 1-2, 5, 10, 14)
    A. The charge of subverting (upset; overthrow; or destroy) our nation
    B. The charge of opposing taxes to Caesar
    C. The claim to be Christ
    D. The charge of stirring up the people by His teaching
    E. The charge of inciting the people to rebellion

II. PILATE'S AMBIGUOUS (vague and uncertain) JUDGMENTS
    A. He questioned Jesus. (vv. 3, 6)
    B. He found no basis for a charge against Jesus. (vv. 4, 13-16, 22)
    C. He and Herod became pals in politically correct, unjust rulings. (v. 12)
    D. He gave in to the mob's demands. (vv. 23-25)

III. HEROD'S ALLIANCE WITH EVIL (vv. 6-12, 15)
    A. He came into his old enemy's territory.
    B. He came to see Jesus do a miracle (thrilling).
    C. He plied Jesus with many questions, not one of which had any substance.
    D. He joined with the mob's mockery and ridicule.
    E. He failed to find anything worthy of the death of Jesus.

IV. THE ANTIPATHY (opposition; abhorrence; repugnance) OF THE JEWISH LEADERS AND MOB

A. They lied. (vv. 2, 5)

B. They accused with hot-headed and fiery emotions.

C. They became a violent mob with deadly demands.

V.   GOD'S AMAZING GRACE

A. The cross of evil and torture became the means of saving mankind from sin.

B. Supporting scriptures

    1. I Timothy 2:5

    2. 2 Corinthians 5:21

Lesson 85

"The Crucifixion, Death, and Burial of Jesus"

Luke 23:26-56

I. THE CRUCIFIXION OF JESUS (vv. 26-43)
    A. The Cross
        1. One was compelled to carry it.
        2. Some volunteered to carry it.
            a. A large number of people
            b. The daughters of Jerusalem
        3. One took up the cross with willingness, as the will of God. (John 10:17-18)
        4. What's our command; requirement?
    B. The Crucifiers
        1. The Jewish leaders (Luke 22:66)
        2. Pilate and Herod
        3. The Roman soldiers
        4. All of us (Isaiah 53:1-13)
        5. Romans 3:10-11, 23
    C. The criminals
        1. One insulted Jesus and mocked Him.
        2. The other rebuked sin; saw his real need; recognized the sinlessness of Jesus; and asked Jesus to remember him in God's kingdom.
        3. "One was saved, that none might despair. One was lost, that none might presume."

II. THE DEATH OF JESUS (vv. 44-49)
    A. The hours when history got hope
        1. The sixth hour (12 noon Eastern time)

2. The ninth hour (3 pm Eastern time); He died.

3. Noon to 3pm: What happened in the darkness? Why the darkness?

_____

_____

_____

_____

_____

_____

B. The curtain of the Temple at the entrance to the Holy of Holies was ripped into two pieces. Why?

_____

_____

_____

_____

_____

_____

C. The loving; tender; and sorrowful responses (vv. 47-49)

D. The last of the Seven words (statements) from Jesus on the Cross. (v. 46)

E. EXCLAMATION: What a glorious moment!

III. THE BURIAL OF JESUS (vv. 50-56)

A. Joseph of Arimathea

1. A member of the council

2. Disagreed with the decision to crucify Jesus

3. A believer in Jesus?

4. Requested and received the body of Jesus; placed it in a new tomb – on Friday

B. The women's adoration and plans

1. They carefully designed a plan of action.
2. "As the body without the spirit is dead, so faith without works is dead." (James 2:26)

Lesson 86

"The Resurrection of Jesus"

Luke 24:1-12
I Corinthians 15:1-58

I. THE ARRIVAL OF THE WOMEN AT THE GRAVE
    (Luke 24:1-3)
    A. Their preparation regarding the body.
    B. Their perplexity: wondering; fear; and awe.
II. THE ABSENCE OF THE BODY (Luke 24:2-4)
III. THE ANNOUNCEMENT BY THE ANGELS (Luke
    24:4-8)
    A. The Lord's past teaching (Luke 18:31-33)
    B. The women's remembrance (v. 8)
    C. The message of the angels (vv. 4-8)
IV. THE ANNOUNCEMENT OF THE AMAZING STORY
    BY THE WOMEN (vv. 9-10)
V. THE ABSENCE OF BELIEF (vv. 11-12)
VI. THE ESSENCE OF THE RESURRECTION
    A. It was the message of the apostles and the early
       church.
       1. Acts 1:21-22 – "Therefore, it is necessary to choose
          one of the men who have been with us the whole
          time the Lord Jesus went in and out among us,
          beginning from John's baptism to the time when
          Jesus was taken up from us. For one of these men
          must become a witness with us of His
          resurrection."
       2. Acts 4:1-2 – "The priests and the captain of the

temple guard and the Sadducees came up to Peter and John while they were speaking to the people. They were greatly disturbed because the apostles were teaching the people and proclaiming in Jesus the resurrection of the dead."

3. Acts 24:15 "and I have the same hope in God as these men, that there will be a resurrection of both the righteous and the wicked."

B. It is the assurance of the believer's resurrection from the dead. John 11:23-26 – "Jesus said to her, 'Your brother will rise again.' Martha answered, 'I know he will rise again in the resurrection at the last day.' Jesus said to her, 'I am the resurrection and the life. He who believes in me will live, even though he dies; and whoever lives and believes in me will never die. Do you believe this?'"

C. The most complete story of the meaning of the resurrection is found in I Corinthians 15:1-58.

Lesson 87

"The Two, The One, The Many"

Luke 24:13-35

I.   THE TWO
    A. Their Discussion:
        1. Of recent events in Jerusalem
        2. About Jesus of Nazareth
            a. A prophet powerful in word and deed
            b. That He would redeem Israel
            c. His death, burial, & resurrection
    B. Their Discovery:
        1. That Jesus had been prophesied to come
        2. That Jesus could open their eyes to see
        3. That Jesus could do spiritual surgery
    C. Their Devotion: (vv. 25-35)
    D. Their Destination:
        1. They arrived at Emmaus but made a U-turn to Jerusalem.
        2. Our destination must always be the will of God.

II. THE ONE
    A. Jesus suddenly appeared to them.
    B. Guess who's coming to dinner?
    C. Jesus encounters people where they are, whatever fits their need.
        1. A question (v. 17)
        2. A question (v. 19)
        3. An analysis (vv. 25-27)

         4. Does not the Master, have the right to correct and
            counter the disciples' belief?

III.   THE MANY
    A. The disciples had to listen. (vv. 25-27)
    B. The disciples had to learn. (v. 27; v.32)
    C. The disciples would contact the many by a power yet
       unknown, the Holy Spirit.
    D. The disciples must love all people.
       1. Their hearts burned with devotion. (v. 32)
       2. Why did Jesus break the bread? (John 6:25-40)
       3. What did they do first? (vv. 33-35)
       4. Love is action.
       5. Love is motivated by devotion.
    E. The many would receive what God wants for all
       people.

Lesson 88

"The Final Events and Words of Jesus in Person on the Earth"

Luke 24:36-53

I. HIS APPEARANCE TO THE APOSTLES AND DISCIPLES
  A. Revealed Himself (vv. 36-39)
    1. He granted them peace.
    2. He calmed their fears.
    3. He affirmed that He was the same person they knew.
  B. Related to their humanity (vv. 40-43)

II. HIS ASSIGNMENT (vv. 44-49)
  A. He connected Himself with the Old Testament.
  B. He reminded them of His earlier teaching.
    1. He would suffer, and die, and rise again on the third day.
    2. Repentance and forgiveness of sin would be preached in His name.
  C. He described their mission.
    1. They would preach repentance and forgiveness to all nations starting where they were.
    2. They would remain where they were until they got their assignment.
    3. They would experience someone very special to empower them to preach: the Holy Spirit.

III. HIS ASCENSION (vv. 50-53)
  A. He blessed them before they went up.

B. He ascended to heaven.
C. They worshipped Him and returned with great joy to Jerusalem.
D. They remained in Jerusalem waiting on the power of the Holy Spirit.
E. Acts 1:10-11 records the key words about the ascension of Jesus: "They were looking intently up into the sky as He was going when suddenly two men dressed in white stood beside them. 'Men of Galilee,' they said, 'why do you stand here looking into the sky? This same Jesus, who has been taken from you into heaven, will come back in the same way you have seen Him go into heaven.'"

www.ingramcontent.com/pod-product-compliance
Lightning Source LLC
Chambersburg PA
CBHW060844280326
41934CB00007B/918